gather

WHY GOD CALLS HIS PEOPLE TOGETHER

KEITH DRURY

D1452648

wesleyan
publishing
house

Indianapolis, Indiana

Copyright © 2013 by Wesleyan Publishing House
Published by Wesleyan Publishing House
Indianapolis, Indiana 46250
Printed in the United States of America
ISBN: 978-0-89827-374-8
ISBN (e-book): 978-0-89827-375-5

The Library of Congress has catalogued a previous edition as follows:

Drury, Keith W.
There is no I in Church : moving beyond individual spirituality to experience
god's power in the church / Keith Drury.
p. cm.
ISBN-13: 978-0-89827-311-3 (pbk.)
ISBN-10: 0-89827-311-0 (pbk.)
1. Spiritual life—Christianity. 2. Christian life. I. Title.
BV4501.3.D785 2006
262'.001'7—dc22
2006004337

This book was previously released as *There Is No I in Church*.

To my son, John Drury,
who has taught me to love the church.

contents

acknowledgements

This book was birthed through hard labor. If you think it's hard to read this book, you'll be happy to know that it was even harder to write. For every word in print on corporate spiritual disciplines, there are thousands of published pages on the personal ones. I would never have been able to complete the book without the benefit of ideas and encouragement from the professors and students with whom I have worked for decades. One student who was especially encouraging was Julie Collins, who for more than a year wrote to me on every one of my scheduled writing days to say she was praying for me. Lunchtime conversations, after-class discussions, and long e-mail debates with fellow professors and students have sharpened this book considerably.

Special recognition, however, must go to two colleagues who rendered exceptional assistance: Dr. Steve Lennox read every draft faithfully, always within twenty-four hours, and offered invaluable biblical critiques of the manuscript. Dr. Chris Bounds, a wonderful Wesleyan theologian, added much to the chapters as they developed. My family was more active in shaping this book than my previous ones. My wife, Sharon, suggested changes in the manuscript from a layperson's point of view. My son, David, read the manuscript two times through the eyes of a pastor and provided a test for how the book would be received among small groups and classes in a congregation. My other son, John, a theologian, provided ideas before I even began to write, then twice reviewed the entire manuscript, checking its theological sense.

Of course I must express appreciation to my editors, who take my twelfth draft and still find plenty of points at which to improve it. My publisher, Wesleyan Publishing House, began publishing my writing in 1972 and has continued to produce it decades later. Which brings me to the final person to thank—you, the reader. So long as you purchase my books, I suppose the publisher will keep printing them—and I'll keep writing them. Thanks to you. I believe that, because of you, this book will make a significant difference in the kingdom of God. I pray it will be so.

—KEITH DRURY
August 15, 2005
February 1, 2013

introduction

This book plows unfamiliar ground for most evangelicals. We prefer to focus on individual spiritual disciplines, like those mentioned in this book's companion volume, *Soul Shaper*. Most of us evangelicals just don't get it when the conversation shifts to corporate spiritual growth or corporate spiritual disciplines—those disciplines we must do as a group leading to spiritual growth. We expect to get a holy church by gathering a bunch of holy individuals. We forget that the whole is greater than the sum of its parts. And we forget that focusing primarily on individual spiritual growth is totally alien to the Bible's teaching. In the New Testament, the apostle Paul was most interested in the sanctification of the church—the Colossians, the Ephesians, the Corinthians, and the other groups of believers as a whole.

The church *gathers* to express corporate worship because individual worship isn't enough. And the church gathers because, when we are gathered, we can experience the "corporate means of grace" which are the ways God changes a people to make them more Christlike as a group, becoming a more perfect body of Christ, a purer bride for him.

Some of the corporate spiritual disciplines are similar to the individual ones. For instance, Bible study and prayer are both personal as well as corporate disciplines. But some spiritual disciplines are unique to the gathered church. The Lord's Supper, for example, is a life-changing sacrament designed for the church as a whole, not something to do on your own.

Another reason this book might be surprising for some evangelicals is that it assumes a high view of the church. This book takes the point of view that the church is the body of Christ and that we together are being prepared to be Christ's bride. You will find here the conviction that the church is not optional. It is God's primary means of making his people holy. Sure, the church is far from perfect. But God is in the process of perfecting his church even now. How? Through the collective spiritual disciplines or "means of grace," like fellowship, corporate prayer, hearing Scripture during worship, experiencing the movement of God in our midst, hearing the testimonies of how God has worked among people, receiving the Lord's Supper together, and seeing conversions and baptisms take place. God uses these experiences to transform us so that we—all of us together—come to reflect his glory.

1 the bride

Craig doesn't like groups. "I'm not the touchy-feely type," he says whenever someone invites him to church. "I relate to God one-on-one, like when I work in the garden or go on long walks." Craig claims to be a Christian, even though it has been more than a dozen years since he's actually attended a church for anything other than a wedding. When his friend Josh challenged him on that point, Craig responded vehemently, "I don't need a priest, preacher, or bunch of hypocrites to get close to God; I go direct. Isn't that the Protestant way?"

· · ● · ·

Group Sanctification

This book is about how God changes the church as a church. It is not about things like personal devotions, fasting, solitude, or the other spiritual disciplines we practice on our own, "just God and me." Those disciplines are important for our sanctification, our becoming more like Christ. Those personal spiritual disciplines are widely known (if not widely practiced). This book is about the other side of sanctification, a side we hear less about: the sanctification of *the church*. Just as God uses personal spiritual disciplines as means of grace to change us individually, he also uses corporate spiritual disciplines to change us corporately. This book focuses on this second, lesser-known, means of sanctification, the sanctification of the church as a whole.

Our Father and Our Family

The Bible's story starts with our Father in heaven. But he is not there alone; he is in community with the Son and the Holy Spirit. The story of creation records a conversation that took place before there were any humans to communicate with. "Let *us* make man," said the Lord (Gen. 1:26, emphasis added). Our story begins in relationship, for within God himself there is community. God created us in his image—in and for community. God is a father and we are his children, so our relationship with the Father is in the context of a family. He cares for us personally because we are his individual children, but he cares more about the family as a whole. God doesn't deal with us only as individuals. A family is more than a collection of individuals, even a collection of individuals who are related to each other. It is something much more. The whole is greater than the sum of the parts. If a father, mother, son, and daughter each try to become the best person they can be, that will not guarantee that they will have a good family. A good family is more than a collection of independently good persons; it is a healthy and whole relational unit. The same is true for the church. A good church is more than a collection of good Christians; it is a healthy and holy unit. That is what corporate sanctification is about: creating that holy church.

God Has Always Had a People

God's history of dealing with the world has always involved groups of people, not just individuals. In the Bible, the people of God are just as important as any individual person of God is. In the very beginning, we needed community. The Bible says that it was not good for man to be alone. In fact, the first major section of Genesis (chapters 1–11) is primarily about community and family issues; it is not just a collection of individual stories. Noah's entire family are the "people of God," saved from the flood. The story of Abraham is not the story of one man's pursuit of God, but the account of God's promise to create an entire people, who would in turn bless all nations. From families to extended families to future generations to nations to the entire world, God is always working with a people, not just persons.

Jesus Came for a People

What did Jesus come for? He came to save his people from their sins. He came to establish the kingdom of God. He came to the nation of Israel. He opened up the kingdom to the Gentiles. Yes, Christ died for me—but the Scriptures repeatedly affirm that Christ died for all. He gave his life as a ransom for many. God is always working with a people, not just persons.

Pentecost Produced a People

After Christ ascended into heaven, what did the Holy Spirit do? Was Peter filled with the Spirit as he was praying alone on some rooftop? Was John filled with the Spirit while walking alone by the sea? No. The Holy Spirit came to a community—the church. And that church took the good news to the world so that every nation and people group on the planet could have the opportunity to be included in the people of God. That community—the one to which the Holy Spirit came—still exists, and we are part of it. We in the church are the people of God. God is always working with a people, not just persons.

We're Getting Married!

Let's look ahead for a moment. The Bible tells us that we are all going to a wedding. Jesus Christ is getting married. To whom? Who could be a worthy bride for the one perfect person who has ever lived, Jesus Christ? You? Me? None of us individually is worthy to be the bride of Christ. So who is? We are. Not you, not me, but *we*. Christ is betrothed to us collectively. Like it or not, we're headed for a group marriage at which time Christ will take us—all together—as his bride.

Individualism and heaven are incompatible. Heaven is not about you or me individually, but about us collectively. Heaven is not a place where your wildest dreams of personal fulfillment come true, such as landing a fish on every cast or playing video games and always winning. These are pagan notions of heaven. Heaven is about becoming a people. Heaven will melt our stubborn individuality and merge us together into a group, the bride of Christ. It will be the church that goes to heaven, not just a bunch of individual believers. That is why people who reject the church cannot be Christian. They won't melt. They won't join the bride.

Some people refuse to associate with the bride of Christ on earth, like Craig at the beginning of the chapter. What makes Craig think he'd want to be a part of the bride of Christ in heaven? If he won't join the bride, then he won't get married to the groom. If we thought much about the future, we'd have a totally different perspective on the church today. We, all of us who are part of the church, are being prepared for the consummation of our union with Christ. Two shall become one. We will be joined forever. Jesus Christ, the Lamb, will marry the church, his bride (Rev. 21:2–9). We're getting married.

Washing for the Wedding

The Bible says we'll be a glorious bride not having spot, wrinkle, or any such thing; but holy and without blemish (Eph. 5:27). How can that be? We might imagine that one person could be almost perfect enough for Christ, but the whole bunch of us together? Never! Yet this is our destiny. Is the church you attend clean enough to walk down the aisle to meet Christ? Do you believe today's church is spotless? As I look at the church, I see some pretty obvious wrinkles, don't you? Obviously, something will have to change if the church is to be a perfect bride for Christ. How will it get that way?

Christ does it! The church cannot cleanse itself, but it doesn't have to. The groom will do that. Indeed, that is what Christ has done, is doing, and will continue to do until the wedding. He gave himself for the church to cleanse her and make her holy and acceptable to God as a radiant, pure bride—a church without blemish. In this wedding, God is both the Father of the bride and he is the Groom. Until he is joined with us, he is preparing us for the wedding. We do not have to wash ourselves in order to meet him. He is doing that now. Christ is cleansing the church, sanctifying her, and making her holy. He is not simply sanctifying individuals one by one; he is sanctifying the entire bride, his church, collectively. This is the "sanctification of the church," which is the subject of this book.

How Christ Sanctifies His Church

How does Christ sanctify his church? He does this by gathering and forgiving us. Salvation is more than being forgiven for sinning; it is about joining the fellowship of the forgiven. When we see people "get saved," we witness this work of God. When we hear the testimony of a new convert, our hearts leap and we are changed as a body. God makes us, as a whole group, to be more like him. Christ is always at work purifying the church as a church. He does this through corporate means of grace, such as the Lord's Supper. When we gather to take the Lord's Supper together, God cleanses us. We experience *koinonia*, or community, and through this loving, caring community, we are sanctified. Together we lift collective prayers and are transformed as no personal prayer alone could transform us. We praise and worship God collectively in a way that alters us more than our private worship does. These are the sorts of corporate means of grace through which God changes the wrinkled and spotty bride into a radiant and perfect mate. As we gather as a bride and submit to this cleansing, we are cleansed and prepared for our union with Christ. A few spotless Christians here and there praying on their own will not produce a spotless bride. The bride can be cleansed only when we are gathered together in one place. That is what the church is—the gathering of believers in one place.

Finally, Christ equips and sends us out together to do his work. This is how he changes the world. But as he changes the world through us, Christ also changes us. As we become involved in evangelism and service to the world, we are cleansed. This does not mean individuals going out to do personal evangelism or personal acts of service in the community. Those things are good, but what is even better is when the church—as a church—does evangelism and service. That happens when the church unites in order to be a witness or when the church works together to build a house for a poor family. These things do not change individuals one by one; they change the church *as a group*. These are the corporate means of grace. They are the things God uses to purify the church and make it holy. These corporate means of grace are what this book is about: how God sanctifies the church as a whole.

What Happened to the Church

Why don't we see this sanctification occurring? If Christ is purifying the church, why isn't it spotless by now? The reason is that we resist melting into a group and submitting to the authority of that group. Instead, we try to make it on our own. We practice spiritual privatization, do-it-yourself Christianity. There is a false doctrine of private spirituality at work that downplays anything corporate or communal. It is a powerful and prevailing secular doctrine that makes it difficult for us to believe the Bible's teaching. Privatization makes religion all about me—and not about us. This thinking is secular at best, and at worst produces a spurious pagan spirituality.

The Solitary Person Myth

Why is the idea of corporate spirituality so hard for us to grasp? It is because everything we hear teaches us otherwise. Modern liberal democracies promote individuality over community, the search for our own personal identity and inner authority. We are not taught to respect history or the collective good. We are taught to get what we want, what we like, and what we need. We believe this is the pursuit of happiness enshrined in our political philosophies. Advertisers urge us to "Have it your way," and we admire people who say, "I did it my way." We esteem loners who buck the system and do things on their own. We have been conditioned by our culture, and we apply this individualistic thinking to our religion too. We elevate privatized religious experience and assume that getting closer to God means getting further away from other people.

As a result, we don't go to church to get holy. We go to the mountains. We imagine ourselves in a scene from some old cowboy movie. We see ourselves sitting on the edge of a canyon, all alone, with a beautiful sunset in the background. We sigh, "If only I could be there, I'd be so much closer to God." What we don't do is picture ourselves growing closer to God by sitting in church. For decades I've spent a few months every year backpacking on mountain trails. When other Christians hear about that, they usually say something like, "I bet you really feel close to God out there, don't you?" My answer is, "Well, actually, no. I feel closer to him in church." They seem disappointed. That isn't because they want to actually go backpacking in the mountains, but because they cherish the myth that God is best encountered alone, separated from other Christians. That simply isn't true. Jesus said that where two or three are *gathered*, he will be in their midst (Matt. 18:20). God is attracted to a gathering of his people, not to lonely, snow-covered mountains or beautiful sunsets. There are good reasons to go backpacking, but being close to God isn't one of them. We encounter God most regularly in the company of gathered believers. We modern folk need to shed the pantheistic solitary person myth and affirm that God meets with his people when they are gathered.

The Fault in Our Own Teaching

We can blame Western society in part for the privatization of faith, but it is our fault too. Faith is personal but not individualistic. This book challenges that overemphasis on individualistic faith, even on the part of some popular Christian writers and preachers. Certainly, each person is accountable for his or her own soul. Yet the soul is not without a body. Our soul's body, its true home, is the body of Christ, the church. We are personally accountable both to and within that community. God calls us not merely to be forgiven and have a personal reservation for the "heaven train." Our call is to join the people of God: the body of Christ on earth, doing what Christ would do, namely preaching the gospel, glorifying the Father, and preaching liberty to the captives and repentance to sinners. Books on personal, privatized religion are popular; scan the shelves at a Christian bookstore and you'll see dozens (including some of mine!). For every book on corporate spirituality, there are a hundred on individual spirituality. This book is a beginning to bridge that gap by emphasizing how the church as a church grows to become more Christlike.

Privatization and Sin

The privatization of faith may be more than just a philosophical problem; it may have a sin problem at its root. The human fallen nature drives us to become the master of our own lives rather than submitting ourselves to Christ and the church. Our love of private religion may simply be a lordship issue. We hate submission. We want to be spiritually self-sufficient. We may dress this carnal desire in pious language like, "I rely only on God," but what we are really saying is, "I rely only on myself." Human beings rebel against submitting to authority, especially the authority of a group of flawed humans in the church. Early Americans wrote the Declaration of Independence because they hated submission. That document has become a creed for people in many nations, but especially for American Christians. We want freedom to be ourselves, freedom to do whatever we choose, freedom to have the exact style of worship music we prefer, freedom to design our own religion, and freedom to retain our won identity by refusing to melt into a group. This propensity may be very Western and very American, but it is also very sinful. The gospel of Jesus Christ calls us into submissive community with other Christians.

◦ ● ◉ ◦ ◦

Practical Tips

1. Don't read this book's companion text, *Soul Shaper*, without this book. *Soul Shaper* is about personal spiritual disciplines, not corporate ones. *Gather* is on corporate spirituality and is actually far more important than the other. If you love the personal and private disciplines, remember that they do not exist for your personal gratification; they are meant to enrich you and then send you back into Christian community having something more to give.

2. Don't think of the personal spiritual disciplines as the foundation for this book. It's the other way around. Personal spirituality is nothing more than new-age paganism unless it is related to the body of Christ. It may be great spirituality, but it will never be Christianity unless it is tied to the church. Christian spirituality always begins and ends with Christ, and Christ is found in connection with his body, the church. From God's point of view, *we* is the foundation of *me*, not vice versa. God's history with Israel and the church predates and overshadows us, and we must find our place in that history if we want to find significance.

3. Don't read this book alone. Find someone to read it with you. Or if you're reading the book in order to review it for a class, try to get the class to truly study it together. This book is like a book on marriage, best read with a partner. Read it with others, experience these truths in community, and test them out together. I would be hypocritical if I did not suggest that you submit the book to the church's authority and communal guidance.

Don't judge this book alone. Investigate it with a community and see what God teaches you together.

4. Don't try this at home. This book is not a collection of cool things you could try as experimental, private practices. The means of grace in this book are corporate. They are things that must be done with other Christians. Our propensity to privatize religion is so powerful that some will read this book and get all excited about serving Communion to themselves during their private devotions. Don't! God has ordained a wonderful collection of private means of grace, things you can do on your own to grow spiritually. He has also set aside some means of grace that can be experienced only corporately. Those are the subject of this book. Use this book to strengthen your tie to the body of Christ, the church.

5. Give these ideas a fair hearing. This book argues that God is working to sanctify his church as a whole. This is an alien idea in our privatized world because we tend see the church as a gas station, a place we visit as customers to get a boost for doing the things we do individually all week. We are dead wrong in this. Two thousand years of church history and orthodox theology contradict us on that point. Christianity is not about me; it is about us. Being a Christian means being a part of the people of God. Yes, God wants to change you personally, but more so, he wants to change the people of God. There is no Christian independent of the body of Christ. There can be individual spirituality but not individual Christianity. This book explores how God gathers and changes us collectively. It will not be easy to read because we don't usually think about collective growth. But God will speak to us if we read the book in community. And he will correct our personalized, privatized, individualized ways

and gather us into a tighter relationship with the body of Christ. If we capture what it truly means to be the people of God and not just persons of God, we will be forever altered. And God will be pleased.

Now what about us? What might God want our church to do in response to this chapter? Our class or group? Ourselves?

• • ● • •

Helps for leading your class or small group in learning from this chapter are located at the back of this book.

2 koinonia

Amy and Jason never heard a speaker quite like Mark, who was the keynote at their church's World Outreach Conference last November. He presented the spiritual and physical needs of Haiti in a way that made them both want to quit their teaching jobs and move to the impoverished island nation for the rest of their lives. Within a month, the couple had joined a short-term missions team bound for Haiti the following summer.

The team included a retired doctor, several nurses, their church's pastor, two teenagers, and three other adults, along with Amy and Jason. In January the group started meeting together twice a week to pray, talk about funding, and plan their trip. In June the group flew to Haiti and spent three weeks working at a medical clinic in Port-au-Prince. On the flight back, Amy wrote in her journal: "This trip was the greatest spiritual experience of my life. I've never experienced such love and unity and care for one another. Why can't the church be like this all the time?"

· · ● · ·

The Communion of Saints

Koinonia is the Greek word often translated *fellowship*. But it means more than having carry-in dinners. A better translation might be *community* because the term actually denotes having all things in common or a community of shared life. You can have fellowship without koinonia, but you can't have koinonia without fellowship. The early church experienced koinonia when its members shared things with one another, met daily in members' homes, and took care of one another's needs. But koinonia is more than eating together, worshiping together, and helping each other with chores; it is being one together. It is the communion of saints that we say we believe in when we recite the Apostles' Creed. Koinonia is unity—becoming one family, one church, one body of Christ. It is a means of grace established by God to do Christ's work on earth. When we experience koinonia, we are changed.

Christ's Delegated Ministry

What did Christ do when he ministered on earth? What was his work? He gave himself to preaching repentance, healing the sick, and teaching people how to live. He ministered by providing encouragement and consolation, then urged his followers to change at those points where they were lacking. He provided solace to the weak, acceptance to the rejected, correction to the faltering, and comfort to those who were hurting. He extended help to the helpless, peace to the harried, and, most of all, love to the unlovable. That was Christ's ministry then, and it still is today. But how does Christ do those things now? He does them through the church. The church's mission is to carry on Christ's ministry. This is why the church is called the body of Christ. We do what he did. We are his hands and feet and voice. Together, we embody Christ for the world. Our primary duty as a church is to continue the mission Jesus passed on to us when he ascended into heaven.

Where do people today find teaching, preaching, healing, encouragement, consolation, compassion, solace, acceptance, correction, help, peace, and love? They find them in the church— the body of Christ. Christ himself is still working in, under, and through the church's life, so the things we do as a body remain Christ's work even now, but executed through a different means. Christ finished his work of redemption on the cross, but he did not complete his entire mission. He never meant to. He came to begin that work, and he continues it through us. When we experience koinonia, we are carrying out Christ's mission in the world. We may be having a carry-in dinner, but what we're really doing while grazing on boiled ham and scalloped potatoes is carrying on the work of Christ. We encourage; we comfort; we rejoice; we confront; we worship; we teach; we correct. This is why we have such ordinary things as church suppers and softball games; they give us an excuse to be together so we can function as a body. Do you need Christ to minister to you? Then go to him. Where will you find him? He is still alive and present in the church.

Not That the Church Is Perfect

The church is not perfect, of course. The reason the church is not perfect is that it is made up of people like you and me. We are not perfect—not yet anyway. Even if your congregation includes no one except Christians who have not sinned in the last twenty years, it still isn't perfect. Even perfect people can be immature, can misunderstand others, and are beset by their own past problems and present infirmities. The church is not made up of perfect angels or automated robots but of ordinary people who are committed to carrying on the ministry of Christ. We don't do his ministry as well as he did it, but we do it better than anyone else does. God could have chosen education, medical science, television, the Roman Empire, the US Congress, the United Nations, or even Major League Baseball to do his work. But he didn't. He chose the church. The church may be imperfect, but it is all we have. What alternatives are there? Where can we go to find the perfect community we desire? To another church—will it be perfect? Will you retreat to your family—is it perfect? Will you withdraw into a solitary time with God and find a perfect community there? It may be flawed, but the body of Christ is the best thing God has going on earth. In fact, it's the only thing. This bride may be imperfect, but the Groom picked her, and his taste is good. It is impossible to choose Christ and reject his bride and body, so we join with others and participate in carrying out Christ's work on earth until he comes again. As we do this, we experience koinonia.

God Works in Community

Our culture indoctrinates us to be self-reliant. We admire people who pull themselves up by their own bootstraps. When offered help, we think it's heroic to refuse and go it alone. For hundreds of years, the self-made person has been the ideal in our culture. We are taught to rely on ourselves, not on others. Relying on others is a crutch, we're told. But that thinking is totally alien to the Bible. God teaches us to rely on him, but also to rely on one another. We are to look for help outside ourselves—not within. In the Bible, people who try to save themselves wind up even more damned than the one who simply says, "O God, be merciful to me, a sinner." The religion of the Bible is not individualistic, but communal. Those who insist on being individualistic may fare well in some religions, but not the religion of Jesus Christ.

Because we view the world through the lens of individualism, we often read the Bible as a collection of stories about individual people. We like the solitary heroes, like Noah, Abraham, Jacob, Moses, Joshua, and Deborah. But the Old Testament is not really about individual heroes. It is the story of the groups of people that these heroes led. God calls families, family lines, tribes, and nations. God calls a people. Even Hebrews 11, the great roll call of Old Testament heroes, ends with this overarching truth: "God had planned something better *for us* so that only *together* with us would they be made perfect" (Heb. 11:40, emphasis added). When it comes to following God perfectly, no one can do it alone—not even Abraham or Moses. Amazingly, the writer of Hebrews tells us that those Old Testament heroes are still waiting for us so they can be made perfect! If when we read the New Testament, we tend to see only individuals, like

Peter, Paul, Barnabas, Luke, Andrew, Timothy, we need to adjust our focus from the individual to the collective. The real story of the New Testament is about groups of people—the holy family; the followers of John the Baptist; the twelve disciples; the multitudes following Jesus; the believers in the upper room; and the congregations in Jerusalem, Antioch, Caesarea, Corinth, and Rome. For every individual hero in the Bible, there are a thousand others whose names we'll not learn until the heavenly wedding, when they will be made perfect with us.

The Godhead Is a Community

Koinonia is not an afterthought in God's plan, and it is not a mere method for organizing the church. Remember that God himself is a community—God the Father, Son, and Holy Spirit. As we are sometimes reminded, God is the original small group. The Godhead is our model for community because it is in perfect unity; the three are one. As believers we desire to be so unified that we work in harmony, speaking for one another and acting on behalf of one another. We will never achieve this perfect unity on earth, just like we'll never achieve a perfect marriage. But we work toward it. God is a community, and his community has spilled out into creation through Jesus. God became human in the incarnation. Now the Godhead is an open community, inviting others to join, because we can be joined to Christ. Of course we do not become God, but we are joined to Christ, who is God. Thus, our final and glorious hope is perfect unity with God. God entered into human life so that human beings may enter into the life of the divine. We look forward to union with God in the future.

Much of what we do and experience here on earth will pass away, but community will last forever. Koinonia is a foretaste of the community we'll experience in heaven, which will be eternal. Eternity, for the Christian, is a community of the shared life in perfect unity forever and ever. Until then we work toward that ideal with the same people with whom we'll spend eternity. The kingdom of God is not just a place we will get to visit as some future reward. It is a present community of people who are on a journey to heaven, people carrying on Christ's work in the world. We are the people of God, and we are on a journey together.

A Correcting Community

Most of us get excited about the ministries of Christ. We like the softer side of koinonia, by which the church provides healing, care, acceptance, and love. We might even like preaching and teaching . . . if it is interesting and has substance. But there is a harder side to koinonia: correction. We don't like being corrected. When someone offers to correct us, we respond curtly: "Thank you very much, but mind your own business." Yet correction is the church's business.

We may resist correction by the community, but how else will Christ correct you if not through the church? Perhaps you say, "I get my correction directly from Christ during my devotions." Do you? How do you know it is Christ speaking? And how do you know that you have not ignored some major areas in which you need to change? "I know Christ, and I know what he wants," you say. Do you? How do you really know what Christ is saying to you? Can you trust your own impressions? All the time? Are you that close to Christ and that free from personal bias? No one can know the mind of Christ apart from the body of Christ.

We get correction from Christ through his body, the church. The church moderates those who have overly sensitive individual impressions, and it confronts those with hardened consciences. Some will say, "I love Christ, but I despise the church." Sorry. You can't just take the head (Christ) and discard the body. A religion based on that approach will eventually doom your soul. You will lack needed correction, which is offered only through the church. Christ corrects his individual followers through his body.

Here are some examples: One day a woman named Jackie was having personal devotions and decided that God had approved the fresh, exciting new relationship she had with a married man at work. "God wants me to be happy," Jackie said, "and neither of us is happy the way we are." Jackie needed the body of Christ to tell her that the spirit she was hearing during her devotional time was not from God. Unfortunately, Jackie refused to listen to the Christian community that contradicted her mistaken impressions, and she married the man with whom she worked, convinced that God approved of breaking up both of their families.

A young man named Aaron announced to his Bible school friends that God had spoken to his heart, promising healing from diabetes. "I have to claim my healing," Aaron asserted, "by having enough faith to stop taking my insulin." Aaron needed the church to step up and correct his misapprehension. If Aaron had the correction of the church, he might not have died in a diabetic coma.

Phil, a married college professor, was spending an inordinate amount of time with a young female student, even spending an entire night alone with her on the streets of Chicago during a mission trip. Phil believed he was mentoring the girl. Should Phil have been left on his own to discern God's guidance? Or did God intend for the church to correct his personal impressions about what is right and wrong, innocent and dangerous? Sometime later, Phil was fired because of this inappropriate relationship.

Sure, these are all extreme cases, and almost everyone agrees that the community should step in to correct such blatant misunderstandings of God's will. But the shared life of koinonia allows the correction of the thousand little things we miss in our personal walk with God. God sometimes speaks directly to individuals, but he most often speaks to the gathered church—and *through* the gathered church. A church experiencing Christian koinonia will discipline its members as part of ordinary life together, just as a family corrects its members during the course of normal life. It isn't a big deal. Koinonia is not just the warm feelings we get from compassionately caring for one another; it is also God's way of disciplining individual Christians. You may be reluctant to trust a community with this corrective authority, but you should be even more reluctant to trust yourself.

Real Koinonia Today

Have you experienced true koinonia in your life so far? Some Christians have. Many experience this caring-sharing-loving-helping-correcting-unifying community on mission trips. One survey of more than a thousand Christians asked, "What single thing has had the greatest spiritual impact on your life so far?" After family, the most frequently given response was this: "Went on a mission trip." The result of the survey was the same for both adults and college-aged students. Why would a mission trip do more to change people spiritually than Sunday school, worship, accountability groups, and mentoring combined? It is because on such trips, people often see true koinonia for the first time.

Mission trip alumni remember the unity, care, open fellowship, corporate prayer, love, and correction they experienced. They recall with fondness how they "all loved each other and accepted everybody's differences." They remember how the team worked together in harmony and prayed a great deal each day. Their experience was not extraordinary. It was ordinary koinonia, and it should be the ordinary experience of the church in its life together. Rather than just fondly remembering their experiences, these mission trip alumni should get busy creating a similar community in their church, Sunday school class, or small group. This is what the church is supposed to be in its ordinary life.

Many smaller churches, classes, and small groups do have such a life together. These groups care, share, help, love, correct, and serve together. They do the ministry of Christ on earth. But other churches (both large and small) can be merely a rallying point for people who are looking for entertainment or instruction. People attend these churches as they would go to a concert or a movie; they come for the show and then leave. True koinonia is seldom found in groups larger than fifty. Usually it is strongest in groups of ten or twenty, or even fewer. This is why large churches spend so much time trying to act like small churches by breaking up into smaller units. Their leaders know that the community found in giant gatherings is limited, and people need more.

True, it is easier to find koinonia on a mission trip or by traveling on a pilgrimage with a group. But these experiences should be merely benchmarks, providing an example of what we're trying to find in our small group or Sunday school class. Koinonia is sharing life together in the unity of the Spirit.

How God Changes Us through Koinonia

God has promised to be present "where two or three are gathered" (Matt. 18:20 KJV), and he keeps that promise. The point of that passage is not to say that when we gather, God is then obligated to show up. The point is that in community, God is present. Whenever we gather in his name, he is there. It happens every time. God gathers because we have gathered. We can experience God when we are alone on a mountain, as Moses did. But God never promised to meet us alone on the mountain. He has promised to be present "where two or three are gathered." We encounter God when we gather with other believers.

We cannot encounter God without being changed. God uses the body of Christ to change us. When we meet the church, we meet Christ, and God is present. When we are in community, God sands our rough edges. He provides healing, mercy, and understanding to us through community. He teaches, preaches, rebukes, and corrects us in community. He strengthens us when we are weak, urges us when we are passive, and corrects us when we are wrong. But he does this as we gather together as the church. It is in community that we best experience the presence of God and the ministries of Christ.

Who could remain unchanged in God's presence and in the face of Christ's ministry? Short answer: many. When Jesus was on earth, most of the people who met him were unchanged. They were interested in what they could get from Jesus or how they might use him for political or religious purposes. They met Jesus, but they were not changed by him. Many people today have similar experiences. They meet with the body of Christ, perhaps even attend church regularly, but remain largely unchanged by Christ. Why? Because it never occurs to them that they are meeting not with a group of people, but with Christ himself.

The primary obstacle to spiritual growth today is the same as during Jesus' earthly ministry: blindness to the truth. People shop around for a church as if it were a product or commodity; they are like customers seeking an entertaining concert or movie that will match their tastes. It does not occur to them that this gathering of people—the church—is different from others. They never think of church as a place where God's presence is found and the ministries of Christ are carried out. They go to church looking for something interesting to watch, and that is all they find.

But God wants more for us. Authentic Christians go to church because they know that is where God has promised to meet with his people. Real Christians expect to receive—and give—the ministry of Christ at church because they know that is what the church is for. People who understand the church in that way are changed by it. A church filled with people who see themselves in that way, well, that would be the true church of Jesus Christ. It would be the bride of Christ.

• • ● • •

Practical Tips

1. Redefine fellowship as ministry. If the church has been commissioned to conduct the ministry of Christ, why not take some time to study what Christ did while on earth? What was his ministry? Begin doing these things as you gather. Eliminate those elements of your class or group that are not ministries of Christ, and add those that are missing. Turn your fellowship times into times of sharing Christ's ministry. The caring-sharing-praying time in a Sunday school class is an example of how Christ's ministry is carried out. What would Jesus do besides write down the requests? Do this as a class. Step up to the plate and take on the ministry of Jesus as a church. He ascended to heaven; it's up to you now.

2. Don't think of koinonia as a means to something else. Koinonia is not a means to an end, but an end in itself. We should not use fellowship as a way of bringing in new people, training people for their jobs, or making the church run more efficiently. Koinonia itself is the goal. We don't have to justify fellowship as a means to achieving something else: "If we have pizza, we'll reach more people." Eating pizza together as a church can be a sacred act in itself. If people are drawn in and trained through koinonia, so much the better, but outreach and training are not the goals of community. The goal of koinonia is koinonia. We fellowship in order to fellowship. We share in order to share. Our life together is a goal, not the means to some other, supposedly more worthy, goal. The next time your group organizes a carry-in dinner, don't make plans

to accomplish anything else along with it. Just be the church; don't try to do church.

3. Start a small group. If you read this chapter and realize that something is missing in your life, resist the temptation to whine because the church isn't meeting your needs. Your church is not a Religion-Mart, created to meet consumer expectations. It is a local representation of the gathered body of Christ, designed to continue the ministry that Christ delegated to us. Rather than complaining about what is lacking in your church, start a small group. In your first six weeks together, study the ministry of Jesus in the Gospels by making a list of what that ministry included. Then organize your group to do those things for each other and the world. Watch the transformation that occurs. In about six months, you'll have two or more groups doing this: being the church. If you're not experiencing the koinonia that this chapter describes, start a group and you soon will be.

4. Take a mission trip. Perhaps you'll need to jump-start koinonia in your life by going to a faraway land with a group of Christians on a mission trip or other traveling adventure. Experience the caring, loving, and sharing together as your personal wants and preferences melt into one unified body. Let this become the benchmark koinonia experience around which you later pattern a small group or church experience. Once you've experienced true koinonia, you'll know what you're aiming for in a class, small group, or in ordinary life.

5. Don't rush off after church. People who complain, "This church isn't very friendly," are almost always the same people who arrive for the service precisely on time and leave as soon as it is over. How can you experience the shared life if you merely observe worship as you would a movie or ballgame? Decide that

next week you will stay at church after the service until there are only five people left. Why not? Do you have something better to do? If you answered yes, think about what you just said. What could be better than being where God has promised to be present? What could be more important than experiencing the ministry of Christ from his body? If you don't have an outgoing personality, find a place to sit and observe. Then watch how Christ will come to you. I dare you.

When Christ was on earth, those who avoided him or rushed away in a hurry received little from him. Christ is still here in the body of Christ, and those who hurry off continue to receive little from him. God is present at church, and Jesus is ministering. Hang around and receive that benefit. You might consider having a meal together each week in order to extend the service. After all, that's why we call it a worship service.

6. Spend more time with Christians. If you have been receiving too little of the ministry of Christ, spend more time being where that ministry takes place—in the company of other Christians. We evangelicals are sometimes so concerned with winning the lost that we forget we are supposed to be a loving community that attracts the lost. We sometimes make Christians feel guilty for spending time with other Christians. If we were right in this, we'd have to make Jesus and the disciples (including the apostle Paul) feel really guilty because they spent most of their time with other Christians.

If you lack community, spend time with Christians. Go hunting with a group of Christians, not just to win the one unbeliever in the group, but because Christians love to be with each other and continue Christ's ministry among themselves. Or plan a shopping trip to Chicago or New York with some Christian friends.

Organize a small group to go on cruise together. Get together every Monday night to watch football and eat nachos. Find a way to spend time sharing life beyond worship and Sunday school with other Christians. And don't feel guilty about it. Don't feel obligated to spend all of your time together preparing food baskets for poor people or handing out Bibles at the racetrack. Those things may be good to do, but fellowship is an end in itself, not just a means to some other end. Don't be hesitant to do things that are aimed at sharing life with other believers. And while doing them, minister to each other. Women are better at doing this than men are. But even men can do koinonia, especially if we broaden our thinking to include some activities like the examples listed above. Start soon. Start something. Find ways to spend time with other Christians beyond attending church.

Now what about us? What might God want our church to do in response to this chapter? Our class? Ourselves?

· ● · ●　· ●　·

Helps for leading your class or small group in learning from this chapter are located at the back of this book.

3 corporate
prayer

BECOMING A PRAYING PEOPLE

Travis and Kara were raised in a church that used prayer sparingly in worship. On Sunday mornings they were accustomed to hearing a short opening prayer, a pastoral prayer—which included as many announcements as it did real prayer items—and an occasional brief closing prayer, which was mostly a review of the day's message. When they relocated to Circleville, the couple found a warm congregation to join. They loved the fellowship of the new church, but found it difficult to adjust to the way it treated prayer.

At Circleville Church, there were always people praying at the altar as worshipers gathered for the service, and a team met in a separate room to pray throughout the service each week.

There were often long prayers by laypeople—sometimes two or three—before the pastor prayed on Sunday morning. Quite often the entire congregation knelt during those long prayers! As if that wasn't enough, this new church had quarterly "concerts of prayer," which were basically hour-long prayer meetings. That was in addition to the prayer meeting held each Wednesday night, attended by almost forty people. At its annual business meeting, the congregation was scheduled to vote on a new building project. The meeting began with a full thirty minutes of prayer about the impending decision.

"I love this church," said Travis, "and I believe in prayer and all that. But I wonder if this church is spending too much time in prayer?"

· · ● · ·

Prayer Changes Us

Prayer changes things. It changes others. It even changes the world. We know this, but we sometimes forget that prayer also changes the church. Prayer is a means of grace that God uses to sanctify the church. A praying church becomes a different church. Through prayer we become more like Christ, we take on God's values, and we come to see that God really does reward "those who earnestly seek him" (Heb. 11:6). The less we pray, the more disconnected from God we become. The more seriously we pray, the greater our chance to become what we were called to be: the body of Christ.

Prayer Increases Our Faith

A church that gets serious about prayer has to have great faith. Can a church pray without believing there is a God who hears and answers prayer? No. Corporate prayer is an active statement of faith in the existence of God. How would a church treat prayer if it had only a weak hope that God really existed? Such a church would give little time to prayer. Instead, its members would choose to do something "more worthwhile," like singing songs and giving talks to each other. Even if a church doubted the existence of God, it would probably still perform baby dedications, celebrate births with a rose on the altar, reach out to include new members, try to grow, serve Communion, and even receive new members into its fellowship. But if it truly doubted God existed, it would have a hard time praying much. In an unbelieving church, prayer would be used as a garnish, sprinkled here and there to provide smooth transitions so singers would have time to exit the stage or the drama team could assemble. It would be used to open and close the service and to focus the attention of the crowd, but it would never be treated as a serious part of worship.

In short, prayer in an unbelieving church would be pretty much like it is in many churches today. The church that prays seriously when it gathers states seriously its belief in an unseen God who is always present. If a church service were constructed in such a way that it would be completely relevant and useful even if God did not exist, that service would not be worship but something else. A praying church makes clear that it really believes in an invisible God. The more we pray seriously as a church, the more we will come to believe that God does exist and does reward those who diligently seek him. The less we pray seriously, over time, our faith in the reality of the unseen God will diminish, at least practically speaking. After a period, we too might become an unbelieving church, still going through the motions of religion but denying the power thereof. Corporate prayerlessness increases corporate unbelief. Corporate prayer increases corporate faith.

Prayer Orients Us to Our Source

Some churches would fare very well without God. Indeed, there are churches still existing today in which true faith disappeared long ago. Of course they are no longer Christian churches, but they offer a kind of religion that has all the trappings but no power. The church as an institution doesn't need God any more than the Rotary club. Institutions and clubs can exist without God—including the church. People will give money without God, sing without God, and listen attentively to sermons that support, encourage, and comfort them—all without God. A church could even become large and successful, raising all kind of money, building new buildings, and giving half its income to the poor without God. Religion can become just one more service business, especially in North America and other cultures still friendly to Christianity.

So what can't the church do without God? The church can't *be the church* without God. It can become a successful institution, but without God the church cannot succeed as the body of Christ. The church's aim is not institutional success but spiritual success. We believers have learned leadership, nonprofit management, and fund-raising so well that we can rightfully say,

"We are rich and have need of nothing." But when we do, God may retort, "You do not realize that you are wretched, pitiful, poor, blind and naked" (Rev. 3:17).

We are not supposed to be waging a physical battle but a spiritual one. The weapons with which we fight are not material but spiritual. And the source of our power is not clever fundraising or clever leadership and communication but God himself. When we pray together as a church, we make the statement that God alone is our primary Source. A church that takes prayer seriously will increasingly become a church that believes in the spiritual warfare going on around it. Its members will increasingly perceive the existence of a battle between spiritual forces in which God's resources alone will prevail. Such a church will gradually, almost imperceptibly, reorient itself toward God. When a crisis arrives, it will turn to God in prayer. When important decisions must be made, the church will hold a prayer meeting. When money is tight, the church's leaders will turn to prayer, seeking God's guidance. Corporate prayer changes a church. When church members pray, by practice they actually come to believe our "help comes from the LORD" (Ps. 121:2).

Prayer Unifies Us

A praying church is a unified church. Corporate prayer melts us into one voice and one heart. As believers, when we seriously pray together, we gradually get on the same page with one another. Prayer is unifying, and corporate prayer is a great equalizer. A church at prayer has no rich or poor, new members or veteran members, young or old, conservatives or progressives. When we pray, we all become helpless beggars. When our eyes are open, we have a tendency to look around the room and compare ourselves to one another. We think, "I am on the board, and you are not," or "You are new, and I've been here for twenty years." Looking around invites comparison. But when we close our eyes to pray, we look up instead of around.

In God's presence, our petty distinctions melt away. I may have a position of power on the church board, but compared to God, the brand new attendee and I have the same power: none. I may be able to trump your idea by reminding you that I've been around this church since 1988, but compared to God's longevity, neither the newcomer nor I have any permanence. The church at prayer becomes a unified church. When we say, "Let us join together in prayer," we remind ourselves that unity both precedes and issues from prayer. We join together to pray, and prayer joins us together. The church that prays together stays together.

Prayer Changes Our Values

Individuals have values that are out of sync with God's values. But when we pray, God recalibrates our values. Whole churches can have ungodly values just like individuals can. Churches can collectively value popularity, prestige, success, power, and wealth, just like individuals. Corporate prayer is a means God uses to adjust the church's collective values. As a church prays, God's values begin to displace the church's. We are speaking here of praying seriously, not sprinkling token prayers throughout our gatherings or using prayer as a segue in worship.

The unifying nature of prayer is one reason the church has prayed the Lord's Prayer together since its beginning. No other prayer so clearly illustrates God's values, and praying Christ's model prayer regularly and attentively should, over time, recalibrate the church's values. On the other hand, this may be the very reason so many churches do not pray the Lord's Prayer. Perhaps we fear God's values. Do we resist adopting the "prayer list" of the Lord's Prayer because we prefer instead to focus on our own agendas? Even if we used the Lord's Prayer merely as a pattern for prayer and didn't repeat the actual words Jesus taught, how much would have to be altered in our corporate prayers?

Why We Pray the Lord's Prayer

The Lord's Prayer can't really be prayed individually. It can be prayed personally but never alone because it is a corporate prayer. Notice that it is full of plural pronouns: *Our* Father, give *us* this day, forgive *us*, deliver *us*. If you attended church in a foreign country where you did not know the language, you might still pray along with the Lord's Prayer because the cadence often matches the way we say this prayer. It is a unifying prayer even among Christians of different languages around the world and throughout history. Christians who fear having their prayers become routine could at least pray the Lord's Prayer together once a month couldn't they? Or is this prayer Christ taught his disciples to pray completely outdated? Why do we enjoy singing the same songs over and over yet resist praying the prayer that Christ taught us to pray more than occasionally? There are many ways to pray besides using the Lord's Prayer, and we are right in using them. But we should not be satisfied with the total abandonment of Christ's model prayer. It is the ultimate corporate prayer—and it comes from a great source!

Prayer Changes the World

In the Lord's Prayer, we pray, "Your kingdom come, your will be done on earth as it is in heaven" (Matt. 6:10). This is a commitment to God to do our part in ushering in his kingdom here on earth. Some of the disciples and many of the more zealous in Jesus' day wanted to see him lead a revolution, overthrow the Roman government, and free the Jews from oppression. Jesus countered this expectation by explaining that his kingdom is not of flesh and blood, but is a spiritual kingdom. In fact, his kingdom is far more revolutionary than a mere change of government that would have liberated the people of a single nation. Christ's kingdom is meant to spread around the globe, changing the world from the inside out. So we gather to pray as a church, just as the disciples did, right before the Holy Spirit came; as the Jerusalem church did when Peter was in prison, right before God opened up the gates; and as the Antioch church did, right before they sent Paul and Barnabas to evangelize the world. When we do this, we are doing the most revolutionary thing the church can do: We are helping the kingdom to come "on earth as it is in heaven."

How Praying Together Changes Us

We've examined some reasons for becoming a praying church. Before we move to some practical ideas for upgrading prayer in the church, let's think a bit about how we pray as a church community.

We Pray as Humans

We are inclined to speak of prayer as a spiritual activity, but we must not forget that it is a human act. Prayer is not only God speaking to human beings, but is especially a human response to God's revelation. While there are times that God reveals himself to us during our prayer time, the act of prayer is especially our humanity reaching up to divinity. Because it is a thoroughly human act, we have a good deal of freedom in our prayers, and the practice of prayer may vary considerably from one person to another. There is no single perfect way to pray. The Lord's Prayer may be the best prayer, but it is not the only prayer. Prayer grows out of our individual and collective personalities and from our relationships with God. Even if all Christians prayed only the Lord's Prayer, there would be wide variations in how we would pray it.

We should learn this about prayer from each other. Churches that restrict their corporate praying to only professional ministers lose this breadth of exposure to prayer styles. Why should we train people to only listen to prayer instead of praying themselves? How do we expect laypeople to learn how to pray if we allow only ministers to pray in public? People will learn best by hearing ordinary people like them lift their voices in prayer. It is something like learning a new song. We usually hear a song first, then participate by singing along, and finally are able to sing it on our own. This is how we learn to pray too. When we pray corporately and hear others pray, our private prayer lives are enriched. Perhaps this is one reason so many Christians lack direction in their prayers; they seldom hear another layperson pray, so they assume praying, like preaching, is reserved for the clergy. Hearing others pray—especially other laypeople—teaches us to pray.

We Pray Along with the Pastor

While we need to hear ordinary Christians pray during our gatherings, we also need to hear our pastors pray. The pastoral prayer is a particular kind of prayer. When pastors pray publicly, they fulfill the priestly office by praying on behalf of the congregation. It is a representative role. The congregation listens "over the shoulder" as the pastor prays on its behalf. The prayer is univocal (in one voice), but it is also corporate because the people listen in and follow along. Have you ever heard someone praying for you who was unaware of your presence? Something like that happens during a pastoral prayer. We listen in on the pastor's prayer on our behalf.

But we don't just listen; we also join in. When the pastor says, "We ask you, Lord, to give us guidance on this new building project. Help us know your will," we nod quietly or perhaps even say, "Yes, Lord." Either way, we are saying, "Amen, Lord. May it be true." The words may be spoken by the pastor, but we all join in the prayer and make them our own individually, and as many in the church join this way, we make these words our corporate prayer. So even when only one person is speaking the prayer, we can still be praying. Corporate prayer can be led by one person but we can all participate. Some of the traditional ways Christians have participated in such prayers are by making periodic responses, such as "Lord, hear our prayer," or, in revivalist traditions, by quietly saying "Amen" to affirm and join in with what the pastor has prayed.

Upgrading Corporate Prayers

While the pastoral prayer may be the most prominent prayer in our gatherings, there are a myriad of other prayers that could be taken more seriously than they usually are.

Invocation. The opening prayer, or invocation, could be something more than a device to get people to quiet down; it could become a serious corporate prayer by which the people genuinely invite God to be present among us and reveal his power.

Prelude Prayer. Some churches have a prelude prayer team that gathers around the altar to pray for the service as the people are entering. This creates an anticipatory atmosphere and reminds people entering that the congregation takes prayer seriously.

Offertory Prayer. Our offertory prayers could become true prayers offered to God rather than stewardship promotions directed at the congregation.

Closing Prayer. In our closing prayers, we might avoid reviewing the points of the sermon and offer true benedictory prayers, or prayers for God's blessing, as we leave.

Listening Prayer. We could try to incorporate listening prayer, like the Quakers have practiced for so long. Prayer is not just talking to God, but also listening to him. Listening prayer can be misused individually, but within an accountable community, we are safer in quietly listening for God's voice to be heard.

Litany. Some churches use prepared written prayers that include a suggested response by the people. These are called litanies, and congregations that prefer a more formal worship style use them frequently. Most revivalist churches use litanies only for big events like building dedications or an ordination service, but even less formal churches could probably use litanies occasionally to enrich their corporate prayer life. We might also rediscover the rich tradition of praying the Psalms as a litany.

Psalter Prayer. The use of Psalter prayer assumes that God himself has inspired the best prayers in the Psalms and that we ought to use them regularly, giving priority to his words over ours. Sometimes old ideas are the best new ideas.

Open Altar. Some of us might reintroduce the open altar, a time of prayer during which those wishing to pray about particular needs are invited to pray at the church altar while the pastor prays aloud for the congregation.

Small Group Prayer. Increasingly younger folk have introduced small group prayer in corporate worship. Worshipers move informally into groups of three to six people and spend several minutes praying together.

Concert of Prayer. A concert of prayer is an entire service devoted to prayer. Shouldn't a church have at least one service a year that is dedicated exclusively to corporate prayer? Many of us have such services dedicated to singing; why not one for prayer?

Season of Prayer. Some churches feature a season of prayer in which everyone prays aloud at the same time, creating a cacophony of prayer that sounds like praying in tongues, even though everyone is actually praying in the common language. Anyone listening to such prayers might wonder if the group has gone off its rocker, but the point is not to listen to the prayers but to join in, and anyone who has ever experienced this kind of prayer will testify that something seems to happen "above" the audience as the group joins in. Urban and suburban congregations seldom try this, but it still exists in many rural congregations, especially near the Appalachia region of North America.

Prayer for Healing. Sometimes a congregation may come together believing that God will heal a brother or sister. The Bible even gives instructions for how to do such prayers.

Prayer Meeting. Of course we should not forget prayer meetings, the practice of setting aside one service every week devoted completely to prayer—a weekly concert of prayer. This practice has largely been abandoned, but the notion of a congregation taking prayer that seriously should certainly nag us.

There are other ways to upgrade the prayer life of our gatherings, but these are probably enough to get us started. It would be interesting to note how much time a church actually spends praying when it gathers compared with other elements of our worship. If you made a pie graph of time for your church's services, how much time is spent praying?

Preparing for Prayer

Why do we carefully prepare sermons and songs yet casually improvise what we say to God in prayer? The answer is in our roots. The free church movement of more than a century ago attempted to strip away from worship the things it saw as "dead formalism," replacing them with "true feelings from the heart." At about the same time, frontier revivalism swept through America. As a result, many Americans rejected high church worship and adopted a simpler, livelier approach to their religion. This approach continues to characterize much of North American Christianity; it has "kept the fire" for more than a hundred years. As soon as one denomination slides into "dead formalism," another hot-hearted one rises to take its place. Off-the-cuff Christianity is the favorite brand of religion in America.

However, giving a bit more attention to what we say to God in prayer might upgrade our worship. Indeed, a lot more attention may be needed in order to move away from our prayer-as-garnish approach toward the prayer-as-central approach to worship. That doesn't mean that we need to read our prayers word for word, but we might at least prepare an outline for our thoughts. When Valentine's Day rolls around each February, my wife might enjoy hearing the feelings from my heart scribbled on a half-sheet of paper ripped from a legal pad. But I know she appreciates it even more when I take the time to go to the store, scan the hundreds of Valentine cards on display, read a dozen more carefully, and find the one that is a perfect fit for our relationship. God does not care if our prayers are written or extemporaneous. He does care how much time and energy we put into them. Preparing to pray is one way to upgrade what we say to God.

· · ● · ·

Practical Tips

1. Record the amount of time spent in corporate prayer. Keep a record for several weeks of the amount of time devoted to corporate prayer in your church's worship service or in your Sunday school class or small group. Don't count the time spent making prayer requests. Find out what percentage of time is given purely to vertical praying to an invisible God. What changes would you suggest, if any?

If you are leading others in studying this book, be careful that you do not become subversive or critical as a result of this record-keeping. Do this as a means of discovering what we all have become together—not what the pastor is doing wrong. Perhaps it's best to not divulge the results of your inventory to anyone but your group and then commission all the members to do their part in making prayer a more central part of all they do.

2. Listen better. Transfer the hard-listening skills that you use during a sermon to prayer. When someone else is praying aloud, concentrate on the words and their meaning so that you join in

making the prayer corporate in nature. Consider writing down some of the things mentioned in the pastoral prayer.

3. Expect more. Many ministers and worship leaders resist devoting more time in the service to prayer. Preaching and musical praise are allotted plenty of time in our services while prayer usually gets the leftovers. Why? Could it be that our own expectations are part of the problem? Perhaps prayer gets the short stick because that's what we expect—and subtly demand—from our worship leaders. We'd never be satisfied if the church gave so little attention to music as it does to prayer. And if the pastor prepared as little for preaching as he or she does for prayer, we'd be outraged and say, "I can't follow all that meandering." Yet we accept substandard praying. Perhaps laypeople need to expect more of prayer in our services, and perhaps then we'll get it.

4. Ask for a concert of prayer. Competing to get more worship time devoted to prayer is hard work. After all, that time will have to be taken from something else, like singing or preaching. Yet most churches will allow for an occasional concert of prayer. Request one. Offer to lead it. If your request is approved, attend a concert of prayer at another church and go off what is done there. Or make it a class or small group project. Or make up your own format. If all else fails, you could have a concert of prayer with your class or small group. Simply devote a whole meeting to prayer, then come back the following week and discuss why it "felt weird" or "really changed" your life. Talk about what you learned as a group.

5. Listen to and learn from others. Begin listening more carefully to the prayers of others in order to enrich your own prayer life. Prayer is "catching." You will catch on to a style of praying from others if you're exposed to it. Get exposed, and catch

approaches from the prayer warriors in your church. Ignore distracting habits in their style (such as constantly repeating the word *God* or frequently injecting diminutive phrases like, "We just want to . . .") and concentrate on the content of their prayers—catch *that*. You will become better at prayer by hearing others pray. Of course, you do not want to become a professional prayer listener. The goal is to become a better praying person and better praying church, not just to become a prayer "taste tester."

Now what about us? What might God want our church to do in response to this chapter? Our class? Ourselves?

・ ● ● ● ・

Helps for leading your class or small group in learning from this chapter are located at the back of this book.

4 Scripture

Brooke attends Circle City Bible Church because she likes the church's studious approach to Bible preaching. Though some members use electronic Bibles, most bring a printed Bible with them, and many are well-worn. Some are carefully marked with handwritten notes and underlined verses. New Christians at Circle City Bible are given sticky tabs to place in their Bibles so they can easily find important verses. When Brooke's pastor reads the Scripture before preaching, everybody turns to the passage and reads along.

Richard Smith, a professor-preacher from a nearby Christian university, was invited to speak last Sunday at Brooke's church. He shocked the audience when he came to the pulpit saying,

"Please do not open your Bibles today, but quietly listen to the Word of God—just as the first Christians did."

Brooke was offended. "The reason I come here is to study the Word," she said. "I won't have some priest read it to me as if I were illiterate!"

* • ● • *

Scripture as Sacrament

The subject of this book is the sanctification of the church, or how God changes his church—as a group—to become more like him. For Protestants, Scripture is probably the easiest to understand of all the corporate means of grace God uses to alter his people. While some of the other chapters in this book may take some time to comprehend, we Protestants already believe deeply in the power of the Word of God. We believe that when Scripture is read aloud, studied, and preached, it changes people. Scripture has power in itself.

The two widely accepted signs of a true church are "the preaching of the pure Word of God and the administration of the sacraments." (Others add a third sign: "And the community is rightly ordered.") Where Catholics tend to emphasize the administration of the sacraments, Protestants have placed priority on Scripture—preaching the pure Word of God. Thus, the argument that the public reading, preaching, and study of Scripture is one of the chief means of grace God uses to sanctify his church will not surprise Protestants. Many Protestants consider Scripture something like a sacrament—a sacred place where God has chosen to meet his people and convey grace to them. While it may not be formally listed as a sacrament in our doctrines, most Protestants treat Scripture as if it were God's chief means of grace, even a more important means of grace than actual sacraments like the Lord's Supper or baptism.

Scripture and Community

Valuing Scripture and understanding its corporate role in sanctifying the church are two different things. In our individualistic culture, Christians are tempted to believe that Scripture is a private love letter directly from God to themselves. Nothing could be further from the truth. Scripture was not written to you or me but to *them* and *us*. Scripture was written to the actual people to whom it is addressed. There really were Corinthians, Ephesians, and Philippians—groups of people to whom the Bible was addressed. Genesis and 1 Kings were written for a nation—Israel. Psalms is not a collection of private prayers and hymns that Jewish people could use in personal devotions; it was Israel's group hymnbook. Philippians is not a letter to a disciple named Philip; it is a letter to a group of Christians in a city named Philippi. Except for a few books like Timothy, Titus, and 3 John, the books of the Bible were written to and for groups of people.

It is not for them alone. The meaning of the Bible ricochets to another community—ours, the church. Paul wrote his instructions on worship to the Corinthian Christians, but we are the secondary audience. The Bible was written both to groups of people living in ancient times and to a group of people living now—the church. Certainly, individuals should read the Bible but the Bible was not intended primarily for individual reading then or now. Almost all of the New Testament is written to the church collectively. If you were unable to attend a family reunion, you might write a letter to be read to the entire family. That letter would have a different meaning from one you might address to your sister alone. Because the Bible is addressed mostly to groups of people, its primary use is public not personal—though you'd never know that judging by the average church.

The Plural You

Because we have been trained by our culture to think individualistically (at least those of us in the Western world), we often read our own expectations into the Bible. Thus, when we read the words *you* or *your*, we assume that they are second person singular: me. So we understand Paul's admonition that "your attitude should be the same as that of Christ Jesus" (Phil. 2:5) to mean that I personally should develop a Christlike attitude until I have the mind of Christ. This is true, of course, but it is not what Paul said. In almost every biblical passage where we understand *you* to be singular, it is really plural in the original language—meaning "you all." It does not mean "you, Jim" but "all of you." So it is *the church's* mind that should develop Christ's attitude, according to Paul. Our attitude collectively should be the same as that of Christ Jesus.

That shift from singular to plural changes the meaning and application of the Bible considerably. Instead of asking, "How can I personally have a humble mind-set?" we begin to ask, "How can we as a church have a humble mind-set?" Consider this startling fact: The words *the, and,* and *in* are the three most common words used by the apostle Paul—which is just what we might expect. However, the fourth most common word in Paul's writing is *you* in its plural form, which shows up an amazing 712 times. *God* comes in fifth with about five hundred uses. The singular *you* (referring to an individual) barely makes an appearance in Paul's writing. Paul was writing to a group, and when we use Scripture in worship, we more clearly get a feel for what it originally meant. We can read the Bible as if it is written to each one of us individually, and that is useful devotionally, but that is not how it was intended to be read. The Bible is written to the church first and only secondarily to us personally. This is why Scripture needs to be dominant when we gather; it is the most accurate way to read Scripture.

The Church Came First

We Protestants tend to value our Bibles over the church. We like to end a theological debate by saying, "I'll read the Bible and decide for myself. I don't need the church telling me what to think." When we do this, of course, we are not appealing to the Bible's authority, but to ourselves as the supreme authority. *We* will decide what it means. That may be why we Protestants hate to hear or read about the true story of how the Bible's books came to be assembled into the Canon. The *church* decided what would be in our Bibles. Oh, no! Every Protestant cell in our bodies sets off alarms when we discover this fact. But it is true.

There were all kinds of gospels and epistles floating around the early church (some of them are still floating around and are easily available on the Internet). A few of these gospels and epistles were helpful writings—at least as good as the writings of Bill Hybels or Rick Warren. But some were crazy and extreme and presented far-fetched stories about Jesus, including stories of his supposed marriage to Mary Magdalene, and some that are even more bizarre. Today, we dismiss these extreme books as silly and spurious. We even ignore the better ones— because they aren't in our Canon.

But during the first three hundred years of the church's history, it was not that easy. What were pastors going to read during public worship? The epistle of Barnabas and the gospel according to Mary seemed to have authority, just like the letters of Paul and the gospels according to Matthew, Mark, Luke, and John. How were early Christians to know which books were reliable and proper for reading in worship? Over a period of more than a hundred years, the church sorted through these writings and sought God's will. Finally, the church came up with the Canon, the list of books that we now consider inspired and refer to as the New Testament. In this process, the church decided to eliminate scores of gospels and epistles from public worship. It did not ban them from being read by individuals devotionally, but it limited what could be read in public gatherings of Christians. The Canon became the official list of books that could be read in a public worship service, with all others excluded. This was a decision made by *people* (guided by the Holy Spirit, we believe) attending church conferences. While we Protestants like to place our Bibles in a position of authority above that of the church, to be honest with ourselves, we must admit that books of the Bible themselves owe their authority to the church, which selected them.

This chicken-or-egg issue is important for us to think about. The church decided which books would be in the New Testament, and the New Testament now instructs the church and prescribes the boundaries for belief. The church and the Bible are not competing authorities; they are corresponding authorities.

And the Holy Spirit who guided the early church leaders to select the Canon is still at work in the church, helping it to rightly understand and apply the Word of God. At the root of this story is the fact that the church, under the guidance of the Holy Spirit, chose which writings would be included in the New Testament and which would not make the cut. We trust them because we trust the Holy Spirit who guided them.

Experiencing Scripture in Community

Most Christians believe that Scripture has the power to change lives. We know this because we have experienced it. We have read verses at some time and heard God whisper, "This is for you; you need to change in this area." Or we have studied verses and testified, "God spoke to me through that verse and said I should trust him and wait a little bit longer for an answer to my prayer." Or maybe we were discouraged and about to quit our work as a youth sponsor or Sunday school teacher, then read a psalm and sensed God saying, "Do not waver but be strong and of good courage," so we decided to stick with it for another year. We are familiar with such experiences, and we know God uses Scripture to convict, guide, and change us personally like this through the Scriptures.

But we're less familiar with how God changes his church, as a group, through Scripture. That is the point of this chapter—the corporate sanctification of the church through Scripture. We're looking to discover how God uses the Bible to give encouragement to the group, convict the group, and guide the group into the future. There are three primary practices that God seems to prefer using as he changes the church through Scripture. They are the public reading of Scripture, preaching Scripture, and studying Scripture in community.

Public Reading of Scripture

Something mystical happens when the church hears Scripture read aloud. Any parents who have read bedtime stories to their children know that far more happens in that experience than the communication of content. It is the same with the public reading of Scripture at church. When we hear Scripture together, something more than "getting the point" takes place. God's Word changes us. Scripture has the power to convert intention to action; it will not return void. As we listen to God's Word together, we place ourselves in submission to it. We remind ourselves that we are a people of one book and this is what God is saying to us, not a songwriter or preacher. Worship is more than merely praising God; it is a conversation with him, a two-way street. When we move on from our filibuster of praise long enough to hear Scripture, we are listening to God's side of the conversation. Paul told Timothy, "Devote yourself to the public reading of Scripture" (1 Tim. 4:13). He wasn't telling this young pastor to keep up on his personal devotions; Paul told him to be diligent in reading Scripture publicly during worship services.

Traditionally, Christian worship has included three passages of Scripture: one from the Old Testament, a second from the Epistles, and a third from the Gospels. Only in recent times have evangelical churches discarded this practice due to their "pressing schedule" of other things, or maybe because they don't want to be "too formal." By doing so, we have displaced God's Word with our own words—greetings, singing, and announcements. If we stopped and thought about it, what are we saying by doing this? Do we really think our songs and announcements are more important than God's Word?

A well-known television preacher used to tell his seminar attendees, "Never read the Bible to people in worship. If you read to them, they'll go to sleep." What? What kind of people would go to sleep when hearing God's Word? Christian people? It is OK that we have a lot to say in worship. God expects us to praise him and to exhort one another. But he also has something to say, and he says it primarily through Scripture. Certainly, we should give as much time to God's words in our worship as we do to a single song or hymn, shouldn't we? Is three minutes too much to set apart to hear from God's Word? If we do that, we can be sure that God's Word will not return void. It has power and will change us as we listen. Those who have ears to hear, let them listen!

Preaching Scripture

Evangelicals may do poorly at public reading of Scripture, but we do quite a bit better at preaching it. Our Protestant and revivalistic roots have prompted us to give preaching a primary place in worship. Preaching is an aural event; it is an auditory, collective experience. Together we listen to God's Word expounded and explained, and together we respond with a nod, an amen, or perhaps with no outward sign at all but with a collective response of receiving the truth. God uses preaching to accomplish the spiritual formation of his church, shaping us collectively into the people of God.

Not all preaching is about Scripture, of course. Some preachers choose to give interesting chats on pop psychology or helpful tips on getting along with coworkers, but we can be grateful that preaching of that type is dying out. The church is getting back to

Scripture in its preaching. The sermon has no rightful place in worship except as it explains, expounds, and applies Scripture. Helpful hints on getting along with in-laws does not measure up to the preaching of the pure Word of God as a mark of the true church.

When Scripture is preached, God honors it and uses his Word to sanctify the church. Jesus prayed that this would be so in his High Priestly Prayer: "Sanctify them by the truth; your word is truth" (John 17:17). Christ expected his church to be sanctified by the Word, and it is our job to ensure that the Word is central to the message. That's why we call the sermon a message; it is a message from the Lord, not from the preacher. The preacher merely delivers the communication, like a herald. Preaching Scripture has a cleansing effect on the church. This is why we preach Scripture and not the morning newspaper or the latest popular book. It's possible to attract a crowd by speaking on those things, but that doesn't make a church. Regular reading of Scripture is like taking a drip IV; it slowly drips into the spiritual system of a church and changes it from the inside out. This is the promised power of the Word of God.

Sermons are for the entire church, not only for individuals. We preachers sometimes end our sermons with an invitation to personal action, but we know that every sermon calls for a response from everybody. The church hears the sermon as a group and responds the same way. Every time. The response may be either positive or negative, but there will always be a response. The entire church responds to every message. This explains why God is largely absent from some churches. The people have, as a group, quit responding to his Word. They may attend to see if others respond, and they might even pray that someone else will come and respond; but they no longer respond to preaching themselves. As a body, they do nothing upon hearing God's Word, other than giving it the cold shoulder. They watch the preacher in the same way they might watch a quarterback on television. They expect a good performance, but many do not expect to be changed by it. And even more would deny that preaching is even from God at all. They say, "These are the preacher's ideas." Many good preachers have been interred alive in such graveyard churches. There are other churches where the congregation gladly receives the Word of God and happily responds. These churches are changed by preaching. Churches of this kind make great preachers out of their pastors.

Preachers are in the spiritual formation business. We are tools God uses in forming the people of God. God is in the business of making a holy church, and we are his partners. Thus when we preach on stewardship, we are not merely trying to get individuals to tithe but are trying to form a giving church. When we preach on prayer, we are not simply trying to get some people to pray more in their devotions, but we're trying to form a praying people. When we preach on revival, we hope someone will experience personal renewal; but what we're really hoping is that the entire church will experience spiritual revival, all together. While a sermon on marriage and divorce may seem to be intensely personal and private, when we preach on these things, we are instructing the entire congregation about the lifestyle that the people of God collectively should live.

Why is it that many people attend church for decades and never understand this? Perhaps it is because we have finely honed our rituals of response as they apply to individuals but have failed to sharpen the ways that we can respond *together* to

God's Word. We know how to give a personal altar call, but we don't have many rites during which the entire church is supposed to respond together. Some churches today are making gigantic headway in this area by using church-wide programs such as "Forty Days of Prayer and Fasting" and *SoulShift* (Wesleyan Publishing House). In these churches, the goal is to have 100 percent participation in a church-wide effort that will lead to a change in the congregation as a whole. Other churches are crafting response experiences to be used following the message, during which the whole church takes action on what has just been preached. Perhaps there will be more of such efforts in the future, and we will see the entire church respond and be changed. Let's hope so, because preaching is not just a religious speech; it is helping us hear God speak through his Word.

Studying Scripture

The church does more than read and preach Scripture; it also studies Scripture. The public reading and preaching of Scripture is usually done by one person with the rest of us listening and receiving. Study, however, is clearly a group process. In Sunday school classes, small groups, and other Bible studies, the church gathers in subgroups to study the Bible and apply it to life. These groups may have a "teacher," but that person is not a preacher (at least he or she is not supposed to be preaching). In preaching, one person prays to discover what God wants to say to the whole group from Scripture, and then delivers an authoritative message from God to the people. A Bible study teacher facilitates the discovery of what God wants to communicate through a group of people to the group. Just as we trust the preacher to preach accurately on the Bible's meaning, we trust the group to discover the Bible's meaning.

So how can we have confidence that a group studying the Bible will get it right? Won't a group mess up what the Bible says? How can we trust a bunch of laypeople to decide what the Bible means? We don't actually trust the group; we trust the Holy Spirit. The Spirit was given to the church to do just such work. Just as the Spirit guided the church in selecting the Canon centuries ago, the Spirit today helps us understand and apply Scripture. There is safety in numbers. One person might read 1 Timothy 2:9 and be absolutely positive that it bans women from wearing gold or pearls or even braiding their hair. "It is the plain teaching of Scripture," that person might argue. Yet when that verse is brought before a group that is seeking the Spirit's guidance, the group might discover a larger, quite different meaning.

The Bible is not a dead book written thousands of years ago, having no meaning outside the first century. It is living, active, and sharper than a sword. It is God-breathed—not just in the moment it was written, but is still God-breathed. The Spirit exhales through Scripture, helping us understand and apply God's Word today. When there are five or ten people in a group seeking this guidance from the Spirit, the chance of error declines. Sure, even a group can get it wrong, but they are less likely to err than an individual. Perhaps this is one reason Hebrews urges readers to "not give up meeting together" (Heb. 10:25). There is safety in the collective nature of the church because the Spirit moves where two or three gather. This is why we study Scripture in Sunday school and small groups.

Not all Sunday school classes and small groups exist in order to study Scripture, of course. Many Christians today are bored with Scripture. Studying "the quarterly" is left to the senior citizens while the rest of us dig into some hot new book (like this one). Our diet of Scripture is so light in Bible studies that we don't deserve to be called Protestants. This is why the Scripture studies at the end of this book are more important than the words on this page. God's Word should always trump any author's words, shouldn't it?

· • ● • ·

Practical Tips

1. Listen carefully to the public reading of Scripture. The public reading of Scripture is not a Bible study. Try leaving your Bible closed and following along with your ears instead of your eyes. Hear the Word of God as it was originally delivered in the church, as the opening story described. God often gives a different message to the ear than to the eye.

2. Train yourself as a public reader. Why do we carefully prepare to deliver a song yet think that we can publicly read the Word of God with little or no preparation? The early church (in the East) took this function so seriously that it created a separate ordination service for trained readers of Scripture. Offer to read Scripture in your church, and prepare for it. You might even offer to do a three-part reading that includes the Old Testament, the Epistles, and a selection from the Gospels.

3. Listen to sermons through Scripture. You might be thinking that today's sermons don't have much Scripture in them, but you may be missing scriptural allusions. Listen to sermons "through Scripture" by writing down all the scriptural allusions

and references implied or mentioned. Remember that preachers often make allusions to Scripture without giving a specific reference. Preachers sometimes use phrases such as "putting out a fleece" or "sin in the camp" as shorthand for "asking God to confirm his will through a specific sign" or "sin within the church." They don't list a chapter and verse, but they are referring to specific portions of Scripture. Keep track of these as you make notes on the sermon, and compare them with someone else afterward. If you have a group that meets to discuss and apply the sermon, you may be shocked at how many allusions the entire group found. Learn to hear Scripture in the message.

4. Ask the corporate question. If you have a small group or class that discusses and applies the sermon each week, this will be easy to do. If you do not, you can still do this with your family or with one or two people from your Sunday school class or small group. In addition to asking the individual question, "How does this message apply to my life?" ask the corporate question, "How does this apply to our church as a whole?" As you do this, watch how your mind-set will gradually shift toward God's perspective and you will increasingly see his concern for building a people of God, not just a bunch of individual Christians.

5. Decide how often your group will study the Bible. Discuss this matter together and decide how often your class or group ought to do pure study of the Word of God rather than studying a book like this one. The reason the Canon was developed was to ban the study of good-but-less-than-inspired writings from public use. These works were not banished from private use, and many were wholesome and helpful—much like the popular Christian books of today. While most churches would not go so far as to banish all noncanonical writings from public study, a

class or group can at least decide how often it will actually study the Bible—once a year for three months? Every five years? One month a year? How often does it make sense for your group to actually study Scripture together? Discuss this together and decide when you'll next study the "pure Word of God" as a group.

Now what about us? What might God want our church to do in response to this chapter? Our class? Ourselves?

· ● ·

Helps for leading your class or small group in learning from this chapter are located at the back of this book.

5 movement
of God

Ian and Kelli moved to North Carolina from California, where they had attended a charismatic church. In North Carolina they discovered Northside Community, a growing evangelical church that was warm and inviting, and they began attending every week. The fellowship was good, the sermons offered solid Bible teaching, and Northside was a "full-service church," offering programs and activities for all ages, which operated like a well-oiled machine. But over time, Ian and Kelli had a gnawing concern that something was missing. They confided to their friend Scott, "We're not into tongues and all that, but we miss the emphasis on God doing the miraculous things we saw at our former church. Doesn't this church believe God ever comes around and shakes things up?"

· ● ⬤ ● ·

When God Shows Up

Obviously God is always present, but his presence is not always obvious. When we experience an undeniable movement of God among us, we say, "God showed up." Of course we are wrong, technically, because God is always present. However, to us it seems like God suddenly arrived, so we can use the phrase even though it is inaccurate. There are times when God undeniably moves among his people, performs miracles, destroys enemies, guides his church, transforms lives, or melts us into unity so that we can make a decision as a church. This is the moving of God that this chapter is about, and it is what the church needs today.

We Yearn for God's Moving

Most of us hunger to experience God's undeniable movement among us. Sure, God is always present. He is present in nature; he is present in our fellowship; and he is present in the Lord's Supper, but we hunger for more. We want to see miracles. We want God to heal somebody in such a way that it can't be attributed to coincidence or dismissed as "God helping the doctors." We want God to show up in our worship in such a way that the effect cannot be written off as showmanship or audience manipulation. We ache to see God defeat his enemies and free people who are in bondage to sin and oppressive addictions. We yearn for God to come among us and speak to us so clearly that we in the church will know for sure his will regarding some important doctrine or the relocation of a church. Perhaps some would say that we are too much like the crowd that wanted Jesus to give them some miraculous sign. Yet God has acted before in ways that justify our desire to see him move again with undeniable authority.

God Showed Up in the Old Testament

The reason we want God to show up and do these things is that he has done so before. The Bible is packed with reports of God moving among his people. It is true that there are long spans of time—sometimes hundreds of years—during which God's people had to "trust and obey" because he performed no dramatic acts. But the entire Bible suggests we can expect God to sometimes show up in powerful ways.

The biblical record begins when God showed up to create the heavens and the earth. He showed up with a flood of punishment during Noah's lifetime. He showed up repeatedly in Abraham's day with a clear call, a promise, a fearsome command for Abraham to sacrifice his son, and (just in the nick of time) to rescind that command. God appeared to Jacob in a dream, to Joseph in dreams and through Providence, and to Moses in a burning bush. God showed up for his people by delivering them from Egypt and by parting the Red Sea. God showed up when he opened the earth to swallow up some of his own people because of their disobedience. God showed up within a pillar of fire and a cloud, and again by bringing water from the rock to refresh his thirsty people. He showed up to heal people through a bronze serpent set on a pole, and when the Israelites gathered to dedicate the tabernacle (and later the temple) God's presence showed up as his glory filled both worship centers. When the Israelites entered the Promised Land, God showed up once again to part the waters of the Jordan River. And we could speak of the lives of Saul, David, Solomon, and all the prophets for whom God showed up to provide deliverance, perform miracles, heal people, and guide the nation. Throughout the Old Testament, we see that God showed up again and again.

God Showed Up in the New Testament

In the New Testament, God showed up in the person of Jesus Christ. The Gospels give us a picture of the sort of things that happen when God shows up: water turns to wine, demons are expelled, people are healed, the blind see, bread is multiplied, repentance is preached, truth is taught, and people are transformed. We might expect these sorts of things from Jesus, the Son of God. But what of the early church after Jesus ascended into heaven? The book of Acts is a record of God showing up continually. In the first chapter of Acts, we see that God showed up to raise his Son from the dead. In chapter 2, we see that God showed up again at Pentecost. In chapter 3, we read that even though Peter and John had no silver or gold, God showed up anyway, and they were able to heal a man crippled from birth. In the next chapter, Caiaphas warned them to quit preaching; but the apostles prayed to God for boldness, and he showed up. In chapter 5, God showed up by striking Ananias and Sapphira dead for deceiving the church, and fear gripped the church. As a result, many more people believed. Sick people were brought to the church, and everyone was healed.

God showed up again on the Damascus road, appearing dramatically to Saul. Throughout the remainder of the book of Acts, we see that God showed up to heal people, exorcise evil spirits, rescue travelers from a shipwreck, deliver an apostle from a poisonous snake bite, and heal the daughter of a Roman official. Sure, the apostles endured pain and suffering and, eventually, all of them died. God does not deliver his people indefinitely from the effects of fallen creation. But he does repeatedly show up to act on their behalf. The Bible asserts this over and over. Sometimes he shows up when sought, and sometimes he shows up of his own sovereign will; but one way or the other, God always shows up. If someone were to tell me that we shouldn't expect God to show up and perform miracles, then I would have to wonder why God would mislead us by providing a conclusive record of such appearances in the Bible.

Why We Don't Expect God to Show Up

The church today needs to see God move, but we don't—or at least not very often. The problem may be our ignorance of God's history with his people, but it is also our unbelief. The stories of the Bible seem distant and unreal to us. They have become like the tall tales of Paul Bunyan or a fantasy movie. We believe God *could* perform a miracle, in theory. But we don't expect that he will. The Bible has taught us that God shows up and does such things, but life has taught us something different. When a mother dies of cancer, our belief in the reality of miracles wavers. When a son continues to suffer from a chronic disease for years after we fervently pray for healing, we begin to doubt. We've seen too many churches divided over building programs, pastors' personalities, or worship styles to believe that God moves among his people much. We can't believe God will perform a miracle of unity among us, so we begin to search for a church filled with people who are "just like us," accepting conformity as a substitute for unity. We believe God did do mighty things in the past, and that he will do them in the future, but we don't expect him to do so now.

We are like the people of Nazareth: We see few miracles because of our lack of faith. We expect little from God, and that is exactly what we get—little. So we lower our expectations by saying things like, "God shows up only occasionally, so don't expect a miracle." Or we take the even shallower route of labeling as "miracles of God" coincidences like a rainless picnic or a lucky open parking space. Most of us, however, simply expect no miracles at all, or very few at best. We may hope for them, but we do not expect them. When we hear miracle stories, we doubt their veracity and secretly consider them just one more coincidence. Even when we hear hair-raising stories of exorcisms in Africa, we shudder and dismiss them as extremism.

We have come to believe in a God who showed up often in the past but who seldom shows up in the present. At least we still cling to the belief that he will show up in the future, to resurrect us at the second coming. But we may eventually come to doubt that too. This is how believers become unbelievers. We become practical atheists, continuing to attend church, serve on its boards, and participate in its ministries, while secretly doubting there is anything supernatural about the whole thing. This is why we desperately need God to show up today in some undeniable way. We are so full of doubt that nothing will rescue us from it but to figuratively put our hands in the holes where the nails were. We need to see God move in some grand, dramatic, unquestionable way in our midst. Our very faith in God is at risk.

How We Change When God Shows Up

When God shows up, Christians are changed. No man or woman can encounter God and remain the same. When the church collectively experiences the outpouring of God's presence, it is forever altered. Generations yet unborn will be affected by God's moving as the story is passed on and creates an ethos of expectancy within the church. Talented speakers, gifted lighting technicians, and brilliant musicians can manufacture feelings, but these will merely titillate us temporarily. They won't satisfy. Such feelings may seem a genuine movement of God, but are just momentary blips of emotions. When God's genuine presence shows up, we will be permanently changed. Permanence is the mark of a genuine encounter with God. This is why we should urgently seek his presence. For when we experience it as a church, we will never again be content with "church as usual." What are some of the ways a movement of God manifests itself in the church? Here are four things that happen when God shows up.

God Heals

The Bible is filled with reports of healing, including instances when "all were healed." It is true that not everyone was healed on every occasion, and every person who was healed (or raised from the dead) later faced death again. But the Bible repeatedly promises healing and even prescribes the manner in which a church should order a service of healing. God did not go out of the healing business at the close of the first century. He is still the Great Physician, and we can still go to him, believing in a miracle of healing. Jesus came to earth and showed us what

God is like, and he did that by healing people. While healing was not Jesus' primary ministry, he certainly did plenty of it while he was on earth. Our doubts about healing limit God's work, and our unbelief becomes a self-fulfilling prophecy. God has in store more for us than we have faith for. God still heals.

There are churches where God's healing is experienced regularly and the atmosphere is one of expectation and anticipation. There are other churches where no one can remember the last time someone was healed or even prayed for healing expectantly. Which type of church do you attend? Sure, God doesn't help all the people all the time. But doesn't he heal some of the people some of the time? And we all agree there are crooked faith healers who manipulate and trick people for their own personal gain. But counterfeits do not make the real thing unreal. God really heals. Today. Now. Will we expect him to show up and heal in our church?

The Holy Spirit Moves in Worship

Worship does not change God, but it changes us. Have you ever attended worship services where everyone sensed God moving? I don't mean a service where only you felt God presence, but a service where everyone sensed it; it was a "moving of the Spirit." That happened when the Israelites dedicated the tabernacle. After they prayed, the glory of God filled the tabernacle so that the priests could not enter to perform their duties.

Have you ever experienced a worship service in which the leaders were at a loss to know what to do next? They had no choruses to sing or chords to strum. They had no clever words to say because God was talking and they didn't want to interrupt. If you have been in such a service, you know how that experience changes a church for years. It is a paradox: drinking in God's presence both satisfies us and makes us thirstier for more. Going without a drink for long enough might leave us unsatisfied, but over time, the thirst disappears.

An experience of the presence of God in worship can be so powerful that worship leaders will devote the rest of their careers to trying to duplicate it. But they can't. Only the actual presence of Christ is real and lasting. When God shows up, leaders should get out of the way. True, some leaders fear that things will "get out of hand," so at the first sign of "troubling of the water" they move everyone's mat farther from the pool. But most godly leaders do not fear God's work among his people; they fear God. And when God comes to our church, it will be changed for years to come. Do you hunger for such a moving of God in your church today?

God Leads in Decision-Making

God does not always show up in order to make us feel something. Sometimes he shows up in order to guide us. God shows up to help us decide practical things like whether or not to purchase property, when to relocate, or which new doctrine is correct. We make such decisions as a group—as the church. When we have important decisions to make, we do not ask people to send their votes by e-mail or click a vote button on the Internet. Why not? Because we believe the Spirit guides the church *as a group* to make such decisions. We believe that where two or three gather, he will be present. To take a vote on important decisions electronically, we would have to assume that church decisions were nothing more than a tally of our individual opinions. That's not how the church works. Although some churches use congregational votes as a way of discerning God's will, the church is not a democracy; it is run by the Holy Spirit. When we gather, we do not bring our personal opinions to the meeting, ready to persuade others. We come prayerfully seeking God's will for his church, and as a group we seek the Holy Spirit's guidance. We have our opinions ready to offer only in the case that the Spirit confirms them first. Nobody should ever be on the losing side in a church decision, except the Devil.

So when we gather to make decisions, we do not open the meetings with a merely perfunctory prayer. We pray earnestly, seeking God's guidance. If the decision is important enough, we will pray again (and again if necessary) during the meeting, even if only to remind ourselves of what we're supposed to be doing: seeking God's guidance as a group. Those who are irritated about the time "wasted" in prayer need to have their minds converted. Prayer is a better means of decision-making in the church than debate. While the church may follow parliamentary law, it is not a parliament. The church is a body, a family, a bride making decisions with the aid of her groom. To us, discussion and debate are not intended to persuade anybody. They are a means to discovering God's will.

When a church experiences this melting into one mind, it is changed. Such a church is no longer a collection of individuals or local political parties holding various positions. It is one, unified church under the headship of Jesus Christ. Leaders who have witnessed such a phenomenon often spend the rest of their lives trying to replicate it. But human engineering and manipulative leadership can't replicate this kind of unity. It comes from God alone when we gather in what John Wesley called "Christian conference." In a church that has experienced such clear guidance from God, the people will hold personal opinions lightly and temporarily, considering them only a means for finding God's will. Once his will is clarified, they will willingly abandon personal opinions and submit to God's judgment. Spiritual revival can start in worship, but it can also begin in a business meeting—if we expect God's presence in our business meetings as much as we do when we sing or take Communion.

God Transforms Lives

This book has a separate chapter on how seeing people converted changes a church, but we should not ignore this miracle in a discussion of God moving among us. The miracle of miracles is a soul set free, transformed by God's grace. When was the last time you saw God show up at your church and change a life? When a church collectively witnesses the miracle of conversion, it is changed. We are not talking here of a person only receiving God's forgiveness. We are speaking of God's transformative power to change a person's life, actually converting that person from a sinner into a saint—not positionally but practically. Actually changing the person's way of living. Forgiveness is not an observable miracle. What is observable is the transformation of a life. When God shows up and transforms a person, the whole church is altered.

God does this kind of thing. He really does! God can show up and deliver alcoholics and drug addicts so that they no longer even desire a drink or a fix. God can show up and mend broken marriages so that people who have come to despise each other fall in love all over again. God can show up and transform an angry man into a peaceful one. He can turn a malicious businessman into a merciful benefactor. God can turn a bitter and wounded daughter into a forgiving and forbearing woman. He can turn a selfish curmudgeon into a selfless and generous old man. When

God shows up, people change. He not only forgives our sins, but he also changes us. God can change unfaithful husbands, resentful wives, disobedient children, and rebellious teens. God is in the life-transformation business. And when we witness these transformational miracles of grace, we are changed. At least we could be changed if we heard about them in testimonies. Is God changing people in your church? How do you as a church body hear about that?

∘ ∙ ● ∙ ∘

Practical Tips

1. Read about God moving in Scripture. If your church seems to have doubts about God's miracle-working power, turn to Scripture and read again about the mighty acts of God. Read other things also. Start reading stories of God's miraculous work throughout Christian history. Search out testimonies in current Christian magazines and on the Internet. Reading about God's acts, past and present, is a faith-building exercise.

2. Journey to where God is moving. God is always present and working somewhere. Find out where God seems to be moving now, and go visit. Sure, you may witness some extremism (that always seems to show up where God is working), but don't be afraid to go anyway. Take some wise soul to help you sort the wheat from the chaff. Don't take such a pilgrimage just so you can learn how to copy what you see. Go so that you will be reminded that God does indeed move among his people.

If your church has not seen a clear conversion for several years (or even if you have but nobody ever talks about it), take a pilgrimage to someplace where you can hear such stories; let them build your faith. Perhaps your church has never witnessed an undeniable miracle of healing. If so, journey to a place where you are likely to see one, or where you can at least talk to people who have. Don't switch churches; just go there to build your faith and then bring back that fortified faith to your home church. Seeing God work elsewhere might help us believe that it could happen here.

3. Hope for a moving of God. If it has been years or even decades since your church experienced the powerful presence of God's glory—or even if you never have—keep hope alive. Keep praying expectantly, avoiding pessimistic prayer tones. Look expectantly for what God will do in the future, and refuse to whine about how your church may have lost the blessing it once had. If your church has been wandering in the wilderness for forty years, lead it to the riverbank, then step in!

4. Seek a moving of God. If your church—as a church—seeks God's outpouring in worship, his guidance in decision-making, and his power for healing, then you will find it. Ask. Seek. Knock. Don't ask alone, but ask as a group, as the church. There are more seeker-friendly churches than there are seeking churches. Become a seeking church. Seek God's presence and power. Start attending every service with the expectation that this will be the day when God's Spirit moves. Go to every business meeting expecting the miracle of unity that comes when God descends on such a meeting. Don't let healing services be relegated only to oldsters and inconveniently scheduled times; make them central to worship. God can show up unexpectedly, but expecting him makes it even more likely. We don't always get what we expect, unless we expect nothing. But when we expect God to move, he may do so.

5. Share testimonies of God's moving in your life. When God performs a miracle in your life, tell the church. Find a way to do this, even if there is no regular opportunity for testimonies in your gatherings. And when God performs a miracle in your church, tell other churches. One reason there is so much unbelief among Christians today is that testimonies are so rare—both individual and corporate. Find a way to testify to God's work both personally and corporately. This is how God spreads an attitude of expectancy and faith.

6. Test reports of God's moving. The church should test claims that God has shown up, particularly when someone has an individual experience of God's moving. Sadly, some reports of God moving are false, or at least mistaken. This is why the body of Christ is the best place for God to show up and why he usually does so in that environment. It is immediately tested by the experience of those present. The history of the church is filled with people who have abused the idea of God showing up, so it is our job to test that claim while not quenching the Spirit. And although the Bible records many instances of God showing up, the people still turned away from him later. They were changed, but not permanently changed. So the final test of God showing up and of the church being changed is the best test—the test of time.

Now what about us? What might God want our church to do in response to this chapter? Our class? Ourselves?

* ● ● ● *

Helps for leading your class or small group in learning from this chapter are located at the back of this book.

6 testimony

BEARING WITNESS TO THE WORK OF GOD

Burt was raised in a Lutheran church and liked his worship "done decently and in order." When Burt moved to Nashville at age fifty, Elizabeth, his wife, persuaded him to attend a small evangelical church. Burt liked the warmth and sincerity of the people but was shocked at how seriously these folk took their religion. Each Sunday the pastor interviewed one of the members, who told the story of how he or she "came to Christ." In the small group that Elizabeth coerced Burt to attend, the first half hour was spent going around the circle with members relating what God had done in their lives during the past week and requesting prayer for personal needs. Fortunately, group members were allowed to pass when it was their turn, which Burt did without fail every Tuesday evening.

Burt was put off by this preoccupation with experiential religion. At the same time, he was fascinated at how much these people experienced God in the midst of everyday life. And he couldn't deny that God seemed to answer their prayers. Burt always considered himself a Christian, but recently he had begun to wonder if he had missed out on something—something that these people had found.

◦ • ● • ◦

Testimony as Story

Testimony is telling others what God has done. It is bearing witness to God's mighty acts, both in history and in our own lives. We give testimonies for the purpose of bringing glory to God and building faith in others. Testimony has a rich and colorful past, but it has been in decline in some churches for good reason: It is easy to abuse, and those who have seen this abuse fear its return. However, the use of testimony is on the rise in emerging churches and among the young.

Those in the emerging generation value story and narrative. They want to hear what God is really doing in people's lives today. They do not judge truth based on past propositions so much as on present experience. Many younger people are keenly interested in other people's stories, and those stories have an authority for them that rivals propositional truth and hand-me-down doctrines. If we believe that Scripture promises something but nobody anywhere has actually experienced it, younger folk are quick to reject the interpretation as inaccurate. They think the proof is in the pudding of experience, not in denominational positions and statements.

While there are dangers with this approach, it will help testimony to make a comeback in our churches and perhaps become even more powerful in the future than it has been in the past. Preaching and musical worship have dominated our liturgy for the last fifty years. Various forms of the testimony may rule in the future. Any church intending to thrive in the days ahead will have to figure out how to revise or reintroduce this powerful element of corporate spiritual formation.

What Is a Testimony?

If you were called to testify in a court case, you would take the witness stand and tell what you saw. As a witness, it would be your job to report what you knew and let the jury decide what to do with the information. Likewise, people who give a testimony at church report what God has done in their lives. They tell what they have seen and know of God's story. In the Old Testament, testimony was focused on what God had done for his people. Believers recited the mighty acts of God from Abraham through the entry into the Promised Land to give glory to God. Testimony reminded the Israelites who they were—and who God is. In the New Testament, testimony is focused on the apostles' story about the resurrected Lord (1 John 1), but it also includes personal stories, such as Paul's retelling of his Damascus Road experience. Thus, testimony in the biblical sense is bearing witness to the work of God.

The Mighty-Acts Testimony

There are two kinds of testimonies by which we bear verbal witness to God's work. The first is remembering and reciting the mighty acts of God. We testify in this way when we recall what God did for people like Abraham, Isaac, Jacob, Joseph, Moses, the children of Israel, the woman at the well, and Mary Magdalene. When we tell about the resurrection of Jesus Christ, we tell the greatest God story in all of history. We give this sort of testimony to each other both in the church and to the world; it is our witness.

While few of today's Christians have memorized and can recite God's mighty acts as Stephen did at his trial (see Acts 7), some preachers do this in their sermons, and a few Sunday school teachers do it to set the background for a lesson. No doubt today's African-American preachers provide our best examples of mighty-acts testimony. The rest of us should learn at their feet so we will know how to give this sort of testimony. It can be given by any believer because it is the same story for all of us. It is our common heritage. The mighty-acts testimony includes the essential stories from the Bible that tell God's story of redemption and should be taught to every child in every Christian home. This form of testimony recites God's work through all of history. We need to hear more of this sort of prepared testimony—for we all share this history, and the abuse of this kind of testimony is rare. But there is a second kind of testimony which is more risky but quite powerful and life-changing for the church.

The Personal Testimony

The second kind of testimony is the personal testimony, which tells about God's work in our own lives. This kind of testimony differs from person to person. Have you been saved?

How did you become a Christian? Have you ever experienced a miracle? Were you ever bound to an addiction from which God delivered you? Have you experienced a "second touch" by God spiritually? Have you been filled with the Spirit? Has God ever done something in your marriage that changed it permanently? Did God ever provide money or a job for you just when you needed it? These are the sorts of things that we tell about in a personal testimony. We tell about the mighty acts of God that are up close and personal. But the name, personal testimony, is inadequate, because the things we tell about may be personal experiences, but once we share them with the church they are no longer personal; they become corporate property. Once the church has them, God uses them to build up the church's faith. We need to see both kinds of testimony restored to our churches, but since the clergy mostly give the mighty-acts testimonies, we will focus attention in this chapter on the personal testimony. It can be given by any person.

Theology and the Personal Testimony

Not every theology is conducive to giving personal testimonies. Is yours? In some approaches to theology, being a Christian is purely about adopting a belief system; it has nothing to do with personal experience. In this way of thinking, to become a Christian is to believe the right things. The only kind of testimony these Christians need is the first kind, reciting the mighty acts of God. They become Christians when they affirm that they believe the Bible's story as told in the creeds of the church. Such Christians might use the term *believer* to describe Christians because they emphasize the importance of what people believe. Many such Christians have little use for personal experience; it is correct *thinking* that counts with them. Are you in this first group? If so, you may not value the personal testimony.

There is another theological approach, one that tends to value the personal testimony. Christians who favor this approach still value right beliefs, but also value personal experience. They say that it is not enough to believe the right things, but that a person must also receive Christ as a personal Savior and be born again in order to become a Christian. They argue that even the Devil believes, but without also receiving Christ and making a commitment to follow him, that belief is meaningless. Christians of this type want people to go beyond believing the mighty-acts stories. These Christians want people to accept Christ and become a Christian through a conversion experience that leads to a personal relationship with Christ. Are you in this second group of Christians? If so, you should value both kinds of testimony—the mighty-acts testimony and the personal testimony.

However, the personal testimony is about more than the experience of becoming born again. This type of testimony gets at another theological question: How close and active is your God? To some Christians, God is distant and mostly uninvolved in daily life. To them, God has created the world and established its laws, but he seldom interferes in it. These folk advise us, "Don't expect a miracle," because they are convinced that God seldom breaks into history and violates one of his own rules— the laws of nature, for example. These Christians serve God, obey his commands in Scripture, and believe there is an afterlife, but they do not expect God to speak to them, guide them in decision-making, heal the sick, or provide jobs, money, or protection on the highways—or at least they expect such things only rarely. Do you have this transcendent view of God? If so, you are probably unexcited about personal testimonies, either giving your own or listening to those of others.

Once again, there is another approach to the matter. Other Christians view God as being more closely involved in the world. This view says, "Expect a miracle!" Christians who hold this view believe that God is close and active in our lives and that he often answers prayer. They believe God provides for his children and gives them daily guidance and direction. Do you lean toward this more immanent view of God? If so, you probably like the idea of personal testimonies, for by hearing them, your faith in a close-in God is affirmed. If you have this second view of God, you probably believe God actually does play a role in providing jobs, guiding decisions, and sending people your way at just the right time. You see God's hand in your life and you want to give him credit for it, so you frequently give a personal testimony, or whatever they label it at your church. This is your way of telling the church what God has done in your life.

Personal Testimony and the Church

When God does something in our lives, isn't it a personal matter—just between God and us? What value is there in giving personal testimonies in church or in our class or small group? We tell our personal testimonies to the church so that God will be glorified and the community's faith will be strengthened. Just as reciting God's mighty acts throughout history builds the community's faith and hope, reciting personal testimonies of God's acts in our individual lives encourages others to expect God to guide and provide in similar ways.

Hearing a testimony about personal salvation builds our faith in God's transformational miracle of conversion. Hearing a testimony of how God provided for the needs of others strengthens our faith in God's providence for ourselves and our church. Hearing a testimony about the healing of others builds our faith in a miracle-working God. Hearing someone testify about how God delivered him or her from a certain sin fortifies our faith that God could deliver us from that or another besetting sin. When we hear the testimony of a Christian who was transformed after seeking to be filled by the Spirit, we begin to believe that God might do such a work for us. These personal stories prompt us to rejoice and give glory to God. And when we hear testimonies, we can't help hoping. Hearing about God's work in another's life increases our own faith that God might do a similar thing in our own. When we share our testimony, the church glorifies God and its collective faith is increased. This is why we don't keep such experiences to ourselves.

Value to the Individual

Not all of the benefits of testifying are for the church. A testimony benefits the person testifying too. Public testimony creates accountability. When I give a testimony to the church (in a worship service, class, or other group setting) of how God has given me new victory over a particular sin, I am inviting those present to check up on me in the future. Testimonies create a culture of accountability in the church. And there's another benefit: A testimony publicly seals my own experience. Personal religious experience—especially conversion—is a dead end unless accompanied by testimony. New converts who just believe in their hearts but never confess with their mouths lose momentum and eventually lose what they experienced. John Wesley, Charles Finney, Phoebe Palmer, and the whole American revival tradition have taught us that while a personal experience of salvation is necessary, its validity depends on a public testimony. "Let the redeemed of the LORD say this" (Ps. 107:2).

The evangelical church has more recently turned its attention away from revivalism toward political action and missional service, but we should not abandon the testimony without far more thoughtful consideration—and probably not at all if we expect to reach the emerging generation. More is at risk than the loss of this one means of corporate sanctification. The abandonment of testimony in some churches has been accompanied by the erosion of the notion of transformational conversion itself. The clergy thought they were only getting rid of an irritating, lay-dominated portion of the worship service, but after one generation they discovered that they had lost far more. Which went first? Did these churches give up on the testimony and then gradually lose the expectation that God would transform lives? Or did God quit working first so that these congregations had nothing to report and thus the testimony died out? I'm not sure. But I do know that where testimony is practiced, people do expect God to be closer and more actively involved in their lives, and this expectation opens them up to more of God. Would the restoration of the testimony bring back to churches a fresh expectation of personal transformation and of God's activity? We don't know for sure, but it's a worth a try.

How Testimonies Change the Church

This book is about how God changes the church through the corporate means of grace. Hearing a testimony can be exactly such a means of grace. How does God change the church through the testimony? Testimonies build faith and glorify God, but they do something more. Testimonies connect us together in the church. The one who testifies connects with the church as he or she speaks. As gathered members, we connect with that person as we listen. And we are all connected to each other as we respond and receive the testimony as a corporate body.

The work of God is primarily a public affair, not a private one. God's work in your life is our business; it is the communal property of the church. When we hear testimonies together, we take ownership of them as a community. Your healing becomes our healing. We can retell the story to ourselves and our children to build faith and inform belief. Sure, testimonies can be narcissistic and self-absorbed, but if they are emceed properly, they can become a record of the local and recent mighty acts of God and transform a dull and unexpectant church into a lively faith community, eager for God to work among its members.

Is your church a community of faith? Are you expecting God to act? Do you expect people to be delivered from sinful habits, healed, and transformed? Do you expect God to provide and guide? If so, how did you come to expect this? You probably heard about it. You heard people tell how God saved, delivered, healed, transformed, and guided them. You came to believe that God really does such things. The testimony is a door to hope and faith.

On the other hand, if your church expects little from God and assumes that "it's all up to us," the reason could be that your church is not hearing enough testimonies of God's work among people. Is God not working, or are you just not hearing about it? Either way, the situation needs attention. Otherwise, your church may become one of those that never expects God to act in this world. Is that the sort of church you want to be part of?

Abuses of the Testimony

The personal testimony is a powerful means of grace—a channel through which God transforms and sanctifies the church—but it has not been without abuses in the past. In fact, most churches that begin using the testimony as a liturgical element eventually drop it. When professionally trained ministers turn over the floor to laypeople, they risk the introduction of all kinds of nonsense, including heresy. Testimonies can be self-absorbed, all-about-me talks, rather than instruments that bring glory to God. It is common for lay speakers who are unaccustomed to speaking in public to worry that they'll have nothing to say. When they finally get the nerve to speak in front of others, they invariably say too much and take too long. Some have told stories or confessed sins that were best kept private. Others have used the testimony as a power play to elevate themselves and project their supposedly superior spirituality to the church. Still others have presented silly and trivial coincidences as miracles, thereby bringing derision upon themselves and the church. A few have recited repetitive personal testimonies at every opportunity, and their stories have become laughably predictable. Without doubt, professional ministers take a risk when they turn over the microphone to the laity.

Yet we take an even greater risk when we prevent laypeople from reporting what God has done in their lives recently. The Lord's Supper has been abused in the past too, but that doesn't keep us from trying to restore it to a rightful place in worship. It should be the same with the testimony; despite its past abuses, the testimony should be returned to a more prominent place in our churches.

Those who have been turned off by the past abuses of the testimony are reluctant to see it return. But it is possible that we could minimize future abuses by coaching people on how to testify. Coaching a testimony is just as appropriate as coaching a soloist, preacher, or anyone who presents a public service to the church.

And coaching is not the only safeguard against abuse of the testimony. Technology might also help. Most larger churches have developed a way to reintroduce the testimony while forestalling its abuse. By using digital video recording, a testimony can be recorded and edited, shortened to a proper length, and then projected for audiences attending multiple services at various venues. The availability of inexpensive digital video recording technology has done more to bring back the testimony than all the rants and papers of the emergent generation. While this recorded medium lacks the face-to-face element—no small loss—it does seem to provide a solution for some churches that allows them to use the testimony without turning the laity loose with a microphone. When we see God-glorifying testimonies, our faith will be fortified and we will become a people who genuinely expect God to act. When that happens, we are a true faith community.

· • ● • ·

Practical Tips

1. Make a mighty-acts list from the Bible. Most Christians today don't recall events the way the Jews traditionally have or the way the early Christians did, but why not give this a try? If you were to make a list of all the Bible's mighty acts of God, what would you include? Imagine that all the Bibles in the

world will be destroyed someday, and it is up to you to preserve and retell the story of redemption. What stories could you pass on, even if you couldn't look in a Bible? This would be a wonderful project to be done during your personal devotions or on a day alone with God. You might begin by studying Stephen's list in Acts 7 and then make your own list. Maybe you'll want to memorize it and offer to recite the story as a mighty-acts testimony at your church.

2. Make a personal mighty-acts list. What would you list as the mighty acts of God in your life? What has God done for you personally in your life so far? What would you tell your children or grandchildren next Christmas if you were to recite this list to them? What have been God's prominent interventions in your life? This is your personal testimony. It will be easier to share with your family or with the church if you make a list when you are alone.

3. Make a family mighty-acts list. Are you married? Do you have children? Wouldn't it be a magnificent thing to create a mighty-acts list as a family? How has God intervened in your family, including in the lives of those who have died? What are the stories you'd tell? Making such a list might be a wonderful way to spend next Thanksgiving, in between eating and watching football games. How about writing the list in some format that you can keep and recount together every year?

4. Give a testimony this week. Even if your church no longer has a testimony meeting, there may be a prayer-and-share time during your Sunday school class or small group meeting. Use this time to give a testimony along with making prayer requests. Indeed, if these times are packed with mournful prayer requests and contain no testimonies (usually called praises in this setting),

people will eventually lose faith and begin to despair. Faith for praying increases when we hear reports of answered prayer. Next time your group is together, what testimony of praise will you offer?

5. Offer to help produce video testimonies. Are you gifted with an aptitude for using technology? Offer to help your pastor or worship team by recording other people's testimonies. Every Christian has a personal testimony. Find and record them. You might make this your ministry in the church. You could record, edit, and catalog testimonies for use during worship services. Include plenty of testimonies of conversion and other spiritual transformation stories. Then get stories of other religious experiences and answered prayer. Make sure that the speakers are specific about their experiences.

Try to capture stories that illustrate particular points a preacher might make during a sermon. That might include testimonies from people who overcame anger, forgave someone, were delivered from alcohol, saw God restore their marriage or provide for them financially, received guidance for making decisions, or experienced healing. Think of the subjects your pastor might preach about, and get testimonies on those subjects. Then you can offer a list of the subjects to your pastor and offer to help project the testimonies as needed. If your church doesn't have the budget to buy the equipment needed, buy some yourself.

If you develop a supply of such stories, they will probably be used. The demand will follow the supply. Once the church begins using these video testimonies in worship, people will invent other uses for them, like posting them on the Internet or giving DVD copies to new members. But even if nobody ever uses the recordings, you life will be totally transformed by making them. Is God making your heart respond to this idea? If so, he may be designating you to take up this calling.

6. Give a mighty-acts testimony concerning your local church. Have you been around your church long enough to have witnessed occasions when God answered prayer for the church? If so, prepare the story and offer to tell it some Sunday, with your pastor's permission. Such collective testimonies are commonly used during fund-raising campaigns, but they have great value in building the community of faith at other times as well. If you are new to your church or are too young to have witnessed God's mighty acts in your church's past, can you think of someone who could come to your class or group and give this kind of testimony to build your collective faith?

Now what about us? What might God want our church to do in response to this chapter? Our class? Ourselves?

· • ● • ·

Helps for leading your class or small group in learning from this chapter are located at the back of this book.

7 the Lord's Supper

EXPERIENCING THE PRESENCE OF CHRIST

Faith grew up in South Carolina and had always attended a Southern Baptist church. But when she relocated to Illinois for a job opportunity, Faith began attending Community Wesleyan Church. She e-mailed her parents and announced, "I've found a church exactly like our home church in every way." That made Faith's mother feel better about her daughter's move to the North. That security was disturbed a bit last week, however, when Faith's pastor preached a sermon on "Communion Sunday," using John Wesley's concept of Communion as a means of grace. Faith was used to seeing Communion simply as a ritualized remembrance of Christ's death. The notion that receiving Communion properly could actually change a person was new to her. Faith decided to try it last Sunday, and she received Communion with the mind-set that it could actually change her resentful attitude toward her boss. Sure enough, she noted a difference in her thinking all week. She e-mailed her mother again: "Am I just fooling myself with autosuggestion, or did God really change me this week?"

• • ● • •

A Sacrament

The central event of Christianity is the incarnation, life, death, and resurrection of Jesus Christ; and the central rite Jesus ordained for his church is the Lord's Supper, which recalls that event. The Lord's Supper is a sacrament, a means of grace ordained by Christ with an accompanying sign. This book is about how God sanctifies his church, changing it to become more like Jesus Christ. The Lord's Supper is one of the chief ways in which God does that. It is the ultimate corporate spiritual discipline, a rite that should not (actually cannot) be practiced alone; it is a communal discipline. We may come to the table as individuals, but we leave as a group—a changed group. Christians who gather and rightly receive the Lord's Supper together actually change to become better people. The Lord's Supper was established by Christ himself, and it has, throughout most of Christian history, been God's chief means of sanctifying the church. How does that happen?

Re-Centering on Christ

To start with, Communion changes our focus. The Christian church has a propensity to deviate from its focus on Christ and turn instead to other things. If we are not careful, we can begin to conceive of ourselves as something other than the bride of Christ. We can begin to act as if we were operating a Broadway show designed to draw a crowd and get good reviews. We can slip into thinking that we are merely a gathering of people whose purpose is to help each other out and build one another's self-esteem. We can come to see the church as a filling station where people come to get topped off with motivation and wisdom so they can make it through the coming week. We can offer all kinds of programs and classes, as if our purpose were to help people cope with life or gain life skills. Those alternative purposes may be good ones, but they are not necessarily Christian. Any religion can offer classes on how to potty train children or manage household finances. Indeed, any organization can do these things; they are not the exclusive domain of a religion. But only a Christian church can make Christ its focus, and the Lord's Supper helps the church do that. Serving Communion is the most practical way a church focuses on Christ.

God changes the church—as a church—when it partakes of the Lord's Supper. In Communion, God refocuses our attention on the core of our faith: the incarnation, life, death, and resurrection of Jesus Christ. The Lord's Supper gives us no helpful hints for a happy life. It is about Jesus Christ, not us. God uses this sacred meal to shepherd the church back from its wandering into good-but-not-central activities. The church is a community of people who really believe that God became flesh, lived a pure and perfect human life, was crucified, died, and was buried, then rose again, thereby giving us hope for eternal life. This is not just a story we tell, as we might tell stories of Santa Claus or Rudolph the Red-Nosed Reindeer. We really believe this.

The church is not a religion business intent on satisfying its customers' spiritual whims or helping them become better people. While the church does meet people's needs, need-meeting is not its primary focus. The Christian church's primary focus is Jesus Christ. When we celebrate the Lord's Supper, God reminds us of this. We regain our focus on the central event of all of history, rather than on the most pressing need of the week. In the Lord's Supper, we think less about ourselves and more about Christ. That is a good change, and it makes us more like Christ.

Remembering Who We Are

The Lord's Supper changes us also by reminding us who we are as a church. It is an act of identity formation. Many churches adopt practical programs aimed at casting vision, imbedding values, and generally helping the church develop an identity. But nothing can do this more practically than the Lord's Supper. Most families have traditions that form their family identity, perhaps Christmas rituals or little sayings that everyone uses. These rituals and traditions bond a family by reminding family members of who they are. The church's central ritual for reminding us who we are is the Lord's Supper. When we take the Lord's Supper, we realize that we are not operating a service club, musical group, or organization committed to helping people become nicer. We remember that we are a Christian church that believes God became flesh, died as a sacrifice for our redemption, and was raised from the dead for our justification. We really believe this. In fact, believing it is what makes us a Christian church.

Eating the bread is a physical act. We crunch down the little wafer or piece of bread. Some of us may even be embarrassed at the noise of our chewing. But that very human act—chewing food—reminds us that Jesus had a very real, physical body. And when we take the cup, we might hear our neighbor swallow the juice. Rather than distracting us from the sacredness of the moment, that thoroughly human sound—*gulp*—helps us remember that Jesus shed real blood. He was not a mere spirit or ghost who appeared to the disciples, but was a real human being, like us. We are not followers of a cult movie in which blood is painted on actors who only pretend to be suffering. We follow a real God who became a real man and shed real blood. We are followers of the tangible, physical, Jesus of Nazareth, who was the presence of God among us. We believe that this really happened. God became a human being.

Though we may disagree on music styles, church rules, and the doctrines of entire sanctification or eternal security, orthodox Christians all agree 100 percent on the incarnation, life, death, burial, and resurrection of Jesus Christ. This is what makes Christians Christian, and it is what makes the church a Christian gathering; we really believe that these things happened. Every time we take Communion we are reminded of this reality. And the less often we take it, the more likely we are to wander away from Christ and come to see ourselves as a community of another kind. Many organizations can do most of what the church does, perhaps even better than the church does it. But only a Christian church can serve the Lord's Supper. The more we do that, the more we'll be reminded of who we really are.

Real Presence

Communion is not a memorial service for a dead man. Jesus attends each Communion service. He is really there. Of course Jesus is always present where two or three gather in his name. But he is most assuredly present when we have the Lord's Supper. A non-Christian can easily accept the notion of remembering the suffering of a man who lived two thousand years ago. But nonbelievers have difficulty with the Christian doctrine that says Jesus is *present* in our sacred meal—assuredly present. Sure, we can encounter Christ anywhere—in a rock, tree, or desert sunset—for he is present in general revelation. But we regularly seek him in the place where he has promised to be. With the words, "This is my body" (Matt. 26:26), Christ promised to be present whenever we eat his supper together. Christ keeps his promises. Communion is a meal hosted by the risen Lord. We gather as a church as the disciples did in the upper room. We pray and sing and teach, and these are good and uplifting to us. But when Christ appears, we are not merely uplifted, but also changed. Sometimes we feel Christ's presence through the music, video presentation, testimony, preaching, and Scripture; but we should surely expect to feel his presence where he promised to be, in the Lord's Supper.

We must admit that we often participate in the Lord's Supper and don't sense Christ's real presence. Why is that? Perhaps it is because we don't expect it. If we treat the Lord's Supper as merely a service of remembrance for a dead man who suffered great agony, instead of as a place where Christ chooses to make his presence real, we will likely get only what we expect. So be it to us according to our faith. But when we, as a church, expect to meet Christ in Communion, we will. And when we do, Christ's real presence will change us.

You Are What You Eat

Jesus made a shocking statement when he said, "Take and eat; this is my body. . . . This is my blood" (Matt. 26:26, 28). Is it? Are these elements, bread and wine, really his body and blood? What do those words of Christ mean? Christians don't all agree on the answer. Some say the Communion elements change into the actual body and blood of Christ. Others think nothing happens to the elements themselves, but as we receive them we receive Christ's presence along with them. In other words, the elements don't change; we change. A few Christians even consider the elements irrelevant and think we ought to take in the real presence of Jesus spiritually; we don't need the bread or wine at all. However, Christians everywhere, past and present, agree that something mystical happens to the church when it celebrates the Lord's Supper. The church is changed; we believers are sanctified, as a group, in this rite established by Jesus Christ. In some mystical way, the church becomes more the body of Christ, not merely in theory, but in reality. We become what we eat.

Communion is just what the name implies: communion with Christ and one another. Just as Thanksgiving dinner melds a family together and alters its relationships, this meal melds the church together and alters our relationships with Christ and each other. This is why most Protestant churches refuse to serve

Communion exclusively to a bride and groom during a wedding but require all Communion services to be open to the entire believing congregation. Communion is a communal act. As we partake of it together, we are changed. We all eat and drink from the same loaf and cup and all absorb the same Lord. We all leave having incorporated the elements into our physical bodies, and at the same time we have taken in the spiritual presence of Jesus Christ. We are one in Christ; we are his body.

And when we take Communion, we connect to millions of Christians, both around the world and throughout two thousand years of history who have practiced this ritual. In a sense, they all become invisible guests at our table. Communion reminds us that we are the body of Christ on earth; we have become what we have eaten.

Until He Comes

It would be a mistake to think that Communion is only about the past. The Lord's Supper should be more than a look into the rearview mirror of history. While we remember a sad occasion (a death), we also look forward to a happy one (a wedding). As Paul reminded us after describing the institution of the Lord's Supper, we continue eating this sacred meal until Jesus comes. When he comes, where will he take us? He will take us to a great wedding banquet, the marriage supper of the Lamb. Our meal is an appetizer that makes us hunger for that great future feast. At that heavenly feast, we shall eat with the whole family of Christians from every century and every nation, of all languages and races. We shall be one. We will attend that feast as a group, not as individuals. The group is the bride of Christ. Our present Communion remembers the past, but also looks forward to this future celebration in which we shall be joined to Christ. "The two will become one flesh" (Eph. 5:31). We as a group, the body of Christ, will be joined to Christ forever. Every time we experience the Lord's Supper, we are melted more into a common body, the bride of Christ—if we receive the meal expectantly and in faith.

Communion Changes Us

Communion changes us when we receive it in faith. If nothing else, Communion will at least alter the mind-set of a church that practices it regularly. That simple act will cause us to quit thinking so much about ourselves and to think more about Jesus Christ. It will lower to second tier our own concerns, opinions, desires, and preferences. It will teach us who we are as a church— the body of Christ on earth—and will prompt us to act like it. Receiving Communion regularly will also prompt us to look forward to the day when we as a group will be a bride prepared without blemish for eternal union with Christ our Lord.

God changes the church's mind through Communion, but he does more. He changes who we are; he sanctifies the church as it eats. There is a real presence and power in this ritual Christ established. Taken properly with expectant faith, this sacrament will be used by God to change the church. God will change us as a community. We will become more like Christ as a community. The Lord's Supper is the pivot point for the spiritual formation of an entire congregation. The Lord's Supper is the great equalizer in a church; whether poor or rich, old or young—we all come to the table together. And in coming, we are changed.

When we become more thankful for what God has done in the Eucharist, we are changed. In short, God uses the Lord's Supper to sanctify the church. Those of us in the revivalist tradition certainly understand this. We believe that people can go to the altar and be transformed spiritually. They can seek a work of God that will change them, releasing them from addictions, delivering them from bondage, giving them strength to withstand difficulties, and giving them guidance from God. The altar call is only a few hundred years old, yet we believe that God can change a person by this recently invented ritual. How much more should we expect God to change us through the Lord's Supper, going to the altar to experience a sacrament established by Christ himself?

○ ● ● ● ○

Practical Tips

1. Practice Communion more frequently. Some have complained that celebrating the Lord's Supper too often makes it lose its meaning and power. But we do not say this of other means of grace, such as prayer and preaching. Who would say that we should not pray in every service because that might make prayer a meaningless ritual? Would we be satisfied with a church that had preaching only once a month or once a quarter because having it more often would reduce its importance to us? If Christ established Communion as an act of worship and if it really changes us as a church, then why not celebrate it more often? When asked how often Communion should be taken, John Wesley reportedly responded, "As often as you can." Fortunately,

in recent years many churches have restored more frequent Communion to their church schedules.

2. Restore the sacred meal. Originally, the Lord's Supper was a short ritual that was the concluding part of an entire meal eaten together. Many churches have found power in restoring an occasional full meal in association with Communion. Even a Sunday school class holding a carry-in dinner could arrange for offering the Lord's Supper as the conclusion to their meal. This would be closer to the early church's original sacred meal.

3. Try serving Communion in homes. Our penchant for creating larger churches and for ritualizing things has turned the original, intimate, sacred meal into something closer to a mass feeding than an intimate meal. Of course God can still work through dry wafers and plastic Communion cups; God is not limited to working only in the ways that are just like the early church. However, experiencing the Lord's Supper at home or in a home group can be a powerful transforming experience. You should speak with your pastor before doing this (many denominations impose restrictions and limitations on how at-home Communion should be done and who can officiate). But check it out. It may be a doorway to greater meaning and transformation for your class or group.

4. Take in Christ's qualities. The next time your group takes Communion, identify a specific character quality of Jesus that your church, including you, needs. As you physically take in the bread and cup, spiritually receive this quality of Christ by faith. It works! Christ's character is available to us by faith. Feed on him and live! This is perhaps the most powerful of all these ideas. Try it and see.

5. Fast as preparation. If your church offers Communion only once a month, you at least get the opportunity to build up to it

and make it a very important occasion. Do you? If not, find out when the Lord's Supper is next scheduled and fast beforehand in preparation for being fed. Ponder the parallel between being fed physically and feeding on Christ spiritually. If your church offers Communion infrequently, you can invent other ways of making the occasion an important, transformational event.

6. Keep your eyes open. Following the lead of the Roman Catholic Church, Western Protestants tend to make Communion about death, dying, suffering, and sin—like a funeral. In many churches, the mood is somber, and we keep our eyes closed as we focus backward and inward. Try approaching Communion with your eyes wide open, looking around at the people in the congregation and quietly pondering the fact that they and you are the body of Christ, which will one day be joined as the bride of Christ in the marriage supper of the Lamb. Then partake. Communion is not only about the death of Christ, but also about his resurrection and return. Shift your mind-set and see the difference.

7. Don't fear being unworthy of Communion. Some have feared taking the Lord's Supper, thinking that they are too sinful and thus are "unworthy" to receive it. They think they should be perfect before they can receive the bread and cup. Don't be afraid of this. Actually, the person who is unworthy to receive Communion is the one who thinks he or she is worthy. It is true that we should not take Communion *unworthily*—that is, in a way that is unseemly, such as in a drunken state or after refusing to share a meal with the poor among us, as the Corinthians were doing. Each of us should approach Communion knowing that Christ alone is worthy, and not us.

8. Try varied approaches. Encourage your church to try varied means of taking Communion. Practicing a ritual in the same

way every time is reassuring in its predictability, but trying some other approaches can be enriching. Try offering Communion at the altar railing or in the pews. Try holding the elements so that you all can receive them at the same time and also taking them individually. Try using a common cup, then little personalized cups. Use unleavened bread and also a risen loaf. Have Communion at the end of a service and at the beginning. Offer it during a scheduled service and sometimes before the service for any who desire it. Make it a somber event, then try making it a joyous occasion. Serve it alone, and try serving it in conjunction with a full meal. Try it with tangible elements, and perhaps try observing "Quaker Communion" (done spiritually, without any elements). Most churches have folk who have come from all kinds of other denominational traditions. Let them suggest ideas for broadening your experience.

Now, what about us? What might God want our church to do in response to this chapter? Our class? Ourselves?

· ○ ● ○ ·

Helps for leading your class or small group in learning from this chapter are located at the back of this book.

8 conversion
and baptism

Pastor Brent is the best preacher First Church has ever had. He spends up to twenty hours a week preparing his sermons, and his delivery is energetic. More than one hundred new people started coming to First Church during Brent's first two years as pastor, requiring the addition of a second morning worship service. Now, four years into Brent's ministry, the church has added a third service and is considering launching a television ministry on the local cable channel. The only hitch in an otherwise stellar four years of ministry has been the presence of a small but vocal group of folk who keep asking, "How come nobody has been saved around here lately?" Brent seldom gives altar calls, expecting instead that people will decide in their hearts to follow Christ.

"Besides," he says, "people don't make this decision in a single moment anymore; it's a process now." The folks who lament the lack of conversions seem to accept that idea. Yet they still ask, "Even if all these people are getting saved slowly—shouldn't we baptize somebody now and then?"

· · ● · ·

The Process of Conversion

The church is a family that is changed by witnessing the arrival of a newborn Christian into its midst. Watching as the miracle of God's grace saves an individual has an impact on the entire group. When a church goes for months (or even years) without witnessing a conversion, it becomes something less. But when a church gets to see a person transformed, the whole congregation is electrified. The church is then a reproducing body and is closer to what Christ had in mind. Seeing conversions changes a church.

When we speak of the church seeing conversions, we mean something more than witnessing the moment when a person prays to receive Christ. We mean the entire process of conversion. When a child is born, we record on the birth certificate the first moment when he or she took a breath. But the mother and father realize that the moment of birth is just one part of a much longer process, including the discovery of pregnancy, nine months of expectation, physical changes in the mother's body, birth, and naming, announcing, and dedicating the child. Birth is a package deal. Likewise, spiritual conversion is a total package. The process starts when God's prevenient grace draws a person toward Christ and he or she senses a growing conviction of sin and need for God. Like a fetus, this conviction grows until the moment of new birth, or conversion, the instant when God forgives the person's sin and the Holy Spirit enters and regenerates the soul, creating a new life.

The process of conversion begins before the instant of regeneration, but it doesn't end there. If it did, conversion would be an entirely private, personal matter. Indeed, when conversion is allowed to end there, it usually is just a private change. This is why when some people are converted, it doesn't "stick." Something is supposed to follow when a person decides to follow Christ. That is why Christ ordained the rite of baptism, by which new converts profess their faith in the presence of those they are about to join—the church. But even baptism is not the end of the process of conversion, for there should follow a period of study and training in preparation for the final act in the process: membership in the church. So when we speak of the church being changed by seeing conversions, we are speaking of the church witnessing this entire process of God's amazing grace. And when the church sees conversions, it is changed.

We can plan impressive Christmas pageants, quality musical concerts, and elaborate carry-in dinners, but few things will change a church as much as seeing the conversion of souls. When individuals are converted, they become changed people. When the church as a group witnesses such conversions, the entire group is changed. God uses the conversion of individuals to change his church.

So how is the church changed when it sees conversions?

It Causes Us to Value the Gospel

There are so many good things the church can care about that it can forget to focus on the main thing: the gospel. The duty of church leaders is to understand that old saying, "The main thing is to keep the main thing the main thing." Other things are always creeping in and displacing the gospel. When the church sees a person changed by being saved, the gospel takes center stage. It is true that we can't witness the invisible things that happen in heaven when a person is converted, things like forgiveness, pardon, and adoption into God's family. But we can see what happens here on earth, the transformation of a life. When we witness this transformation, we too are changed. And the more we see it, the more different we'll become. When conversions occur, the gospel becomes the main thing again and our other priorities get adjusted. After hearing the testimony of the newly transformed convert, we whisper under our collective breath, "This is what it's all about."

It Unifies the Church

When a church goes too long without seeing conversions, it turns on itself. If a church does not taste the nourishment of seeing souls saved, it will cannibalize itself as people turn on each other. People get worked up about their musical preferences, frustrated by the church's organizational weaknesses, or irate about financial decisions and personnel problems. These issues often yield disagreement, division, and strife. But seeing the transformation of a new convert's life brings unity. We may grumble about music or about the new building plans, but what

117

real Christian would grumble about seeing new converts? When people are converted, the church pulls together. It is not that these other things are unimportant. They matter; they're just not central. When church members see dissension among themselves, they should always ask, "When was the last time we saw the conversion of a lost soul?"

It Increases Our Corporate Faith

Faith is not just an individual phenomenon; it is a communal thing. Groups can have faith together, and they can have corporate unbelief. The people of Nazareth were just such a group. They possessed a collective unbelief about Jesus, and it limited what he was able to do among them. There are many Nazareth churches. These are churches that have developed a collective ethos of unbelief. Like the people of Nazareth, these churches don't expect much from God, and they don't get much. Their unbelief becomes a vicious cycle: The people see no miracles, so they expect no miracles, so they receive no miracles, and so on.

But there is another kind of church. These churches are characterized by collective faith. The atmosphere among them is electric and expectant. The people there wait for God to act with bated breath, and he often does. This corporate faith initiates a cycle of the opposite kind: The people expect God to respond, and God does respond, so the people continue to be expectant which invites even greater response from God, and so on. This is why some churches constantly experience God's work while for others, the glory has departed.

Most of us in the church constantly wrestle with unbelief. It isn't that we lack belief in God, but we struggle to believe that he does much in the world today. Without intervention, many of us will become practical atheists, expecting God to do less and less until he eventually does nothing whatsoever. We elevate him out of daily life and assign him to the heavens, where he watches human life from a distance. As unbelief makes advances in our lives, we may come to privately doubt God's very existence—or may at least wonder if he really cares about us. Entire congregations can descend into such unbelief even as they gather consistently to worship. They may go through the motions of worshiping a distant and remote God who shows up only seldom—or never.

The remedy for such unbelief is to witness a miraculous conversion, one by which someone's life is dramatically changed. When we see God rescue a sinner, changing that person's desires, perhaps delivering him or her from addictions or mending a marriage, our faith leaps. We escape Nazareth unbelief and become an expectant community. God becomes real to us again; he becomes near again. All this happens when we see God convert a person in our midst. As God transforms a sinner into a saint, he also transforms the church into a community of faith and expectancy. After all, the "miracle of miracles" is the transformation of a human life.

It Reminds Us That We Are a Family

It is easy for us as a church to forget what we really are. We are not a service club, drama troupe, or social service agency. We are a family. As a family, we should reproduce, giving birth to new children. When a family experiences a birth, everyone rushes to the hospital, takes pictures, sends out announcements, and gives away cigars to celebrate. (Well, maybe bubble gum cigars at least.) When the church has a birth, we should do likewise.

A new convert adds to our family, and we should celebrate! Everyone knows that newborns demand a lot of care and can be troublesome. Even so, a family gets excited about the birth and bands together to provide the nurture and care the child needs. In the same way, a new birth at the church reminds us how we must work together as a family. All at once we understand why we have Sunday school, and small groups, and membership training: The newborns need help. We may yawn our way through these meetings, but when a new convert comes along, we see that such meetings offer life-sustaining substance for spiritual newborns.

Churches that see conversions frequently act more like a family. These churches have the energy of a young family busily arranging car seats for a trip to the grocery store. Unfortunately, other churches are empty nest churches; their newborns of yesteryear have all grown up and moved away. These churches long ago went through evangelistic menopause. Churches like these forget they are supposed to reproduce. They become gatherings of grouches. None of this is tied to the chronological age of a congregation. The church of Jesus Christ is several thousand years old and can still give birth. A church should never outlive childbearing years. If we're not seeing new converts, either we are practicing spiritual birth control (abstinence from evangelism) or we've simply forgotten how new ones are made.

It Moves Us Emotionally

Giving birth is an emotional experience. Mothers cry tears of joy and feel emotions they've never felt before when holding their first-born child. New fathers become emotional too. They may call their mothers and thank them for all they've done, or they may just faint and fall to the floor. A new birth affects us emotionally. We feel something. Human beings need feelings. We long to be moved emotionally. That's why we watch tear-jerker movies and ride roller coasters. "I feel, therefore I am" might be the motto for the modern human race. Feeling tells us that we are alive. This quest to experience feelings can lead to problems, but it still makes sense that we ought to feel something in our religion, doesn't it? Would we want a marriage devoid of feelings? Of course not! And most of us don't want our religion all locked up in our heads, with no connection to the heart.

So where do we get our feelings at church? For many, feelings are experienced through music. Young people can stand and sing for an hour (or at least it seems that long to the older folk). The reason they do that is to feel something. They sense God's presence in the music. We all ought to feel something in worship.

The church ought to create more opportunities to experience feelings, especially through avenues beyond musical praise. How about letting the church witness a new birth? Let us all see the miracle! Let us hear the testimony of a new convert, and as we do, our hearts will leap—not just our individual hearts, but also the collective heart of the congregation. Tears will come to eyes. Grins will form at the corners of mouths. Lumps will rise in throats. Something inside us, very near to our hearts, will be moved. When churchgoers see a conversion, they feel something. They do if they are part of the family, that is. Those who don't respond with joy at a new birth are strangers and not truly part of the family. They need to be born into the family themselves. The rest of us feel God's presence when we see the miracle of new birth, which is precisely why we need to see it.

It Changes How We Look at the Church

Whether we know it or not, many of us treat the church as if it were a religious business and assume that we are its customers. We expect to be provided with products and services that satisfy our needs and meet our exacting standards. We expect our complaints to be heard and responded to by a customer service representative—usually the pastor. And if we don't get what we want, we will simply "shop" elsewhere. This is the American view of the church. And it is wrong.

Witnessing conversions reminds us how wrong this consumerist thinking is. The less often we see people saved, the more likely we are to expect the church to exist for our generation and to meet our needs. The more often we witness conversions, the more we'll come to see the church as a grand, historic body, thousands of years old, that exists to pass on the faith from generation to generation. When we witness conversions, we see that the church is not about us but about her, him, and them. And we will make the church less about our own generation and more about the next one. When we become eyewitnesses to the transformed lives of new converts, we realize the often-stated truths that "it's not about me" and "it's not about us." We come to see ourselves as one link in a long chain extending from the resurrection of Jesus Christ to the second coming, with each link passing on the faith from one generation to the next. We become servers, not consumers. A church without conversions gets preoccupied with itself and with the present day. A church seeing new births will be more concerned with others and with the future. God uses new births to turn the church's focus inside out.

It Teaches Us Who We Are

All conversions should culminate in baptism. When they do, we learn better who we are, both as individuals and as a church. While conversion can happen in private as a result of personal evangelism, baptism is always public. It is the sacrament ordained by Christ to make conversion a public matter. And it changes the person baptized. Just as something really happens when we are saved, something really happens when we are baptized. Baptism is a means of grace, meaning that God actually works in us when we obediently submit to him through this ritual. It is, therefore, much more than an external ritual; it is a real act of the Spirit.

Baptism changes not only the person baptized, but also the entire church. Baptism also teaches us. This rite reminds us of our identity. It is the rite of initiation into the church of Jesus Christ, and it has been since the church began. Preaching is the audible symbol that points toward the gospel, and baptism is the visible symbol. When combined, they both proclaim and demonstrate that the gospel is the power of God for salvation. When we witness a baptism, we participate in a ritual of induction. It is true, technically speaking, that the new convert was saved when he or she prayed the prayer at the altar or in someone's living room. But that person is publicly received into the body of Christ when he or she submits to baptism. We invented the altar call a little over two hundred years ago, but Jesus Christ ordained baptism more than two thousand years ago.

Baptism is a public affair. There is no such thing as secret discipleship. When people try to follow Jesus in secret, one of two things eventually happens. Either their following of Jesus eliminates their secrecy, or their secrecy eliminates their following of

Christ. Baptism makes conversion public. At baptism, conversion becomes everybody's business. This ritual alerts us to the fact that there has been a birth and reminds us that we should try to help the new convert grow. If a tree falls in the woods and nobody hears it, does it make a sound? That old question might be asked about conversion. If a person is converted but nobody ever hears of it, does that conversion have an impact on the spiritual formation of the church? While a private conversion might have value to the individual or to the soul winner, it means as little to the church as does a fallen tree in the woods. It is true that an altar call followed by a testimony to conversion is an effective means of making conversions public. But baptism is even more effective. Every church needs some means of making conversion a family matter. The rite Christ established for public confession of faith and entry into the church is baptism. We will never invent a better one.

• • ● • •

Practical Tips

1. Develop a strategy for seeing conversion in your church. This chapter claims that the church—as a church—needs to witness at least part of the conversion process in order to be changed. How does your church do this? What might improve your church's practice? When was the most recent conversion your church has experienced? When was the last time someone was baptized?

2. Record dates of baptisms. While every Christian may not be able to cite the date of his or her conversion, we all should be

able to cite the date of our baptism. There is no such thing as a gradual baptism; it is a line to cross. How can the church make this date seem more important? Some churches present baptismal certificates or mementos to the newly baptized. Some parents buy a plaque and have it inscribed with the date of their child's conversion and baptism, then display the plaque in the child's room. What ideas do you have for ways a church (or parents or small group) can help people remember their conversion and baptism?

3. Include testimonies with baptisms. Making a verbal confession of faith and briefly relating the story of how a new convert came to Christ is a more powerful message than what preachers can deliver. It is customary to make this testimony at baptism; though in churches that practice public altar calls, the testimony sometimes immediately follows praying at the altar. In what setting does your church provide for personal testimonies of conversion? What might improve your church's practice?

4. Have group baptisms. Many churches baptize people in groups on a single day, just as the early church did. The idea is not just to be more efficient or to save money on heating the baptismal pool. The idea is to remind us that though we are saved individually, we are saved into a community. Baptism is a communal act. Like Communion, it is not to be done alone. You wouldn't serve the Lord's Supper to yourself alone, and you shouldn't baptize yourself either. Baptism involves both the new convert and the body into which the convert is received.

5. Recall your own conversion and baptism. When someone else is converted or baptized, remember your own conversion and baptism as a means of affirming who you are. As Christians, our primary identity is never found in remembering our wedding,

graduation ceremony, or the date on which we became citizens of an earthly nation; it is found in our conversion and baptism. This is the defining event in the life of a Christian. Just as couples remember their wedding and may privately reaffirm their vows while attending another's wedding, so witnessing a conversion or baptism should make us recall and confirm our own conversion and baptism. Learn to practice this recollection at every baptism you witness in the future. When were you saved? Tell someone about it. Then tell about your baptism.

6. Let baptism melt distinctions. Praying aloud in front of a whole congregation can be very humbling. Baptism is even more humbling, especially baptism by immersion. We go before a fully dressed and coiffed congregation and are dunked into the water. We come out sputtering and sopping wet. No wonder outsiders see this rite as something like a fraternity initiation. Yet that fraternal aspect is the genius of this experience; we all got wet. Baptism demolishes any distinction between old-timers and newcomers; we all went through this at one time or another. There is not a separate rite for men and women (as there was in Judaism's circumcision). In baptism we are all equal, and the water treats us uniformly. The rich woman's hair winds up in the same matted mess as the store clerk's. Gentile and Jewish Christians, rich and poor, slave and free, male and female "all get wet" in baptism (Gal. 3:27–28 was a baptism formula in the early church). The next time your church has a baptism service, remind your friends to think of baptism this way. Remind yourself that the newly baptized person is joining the community on an absolutely egalitarian basis. What other practices in the church could help you understand the equality of all believers?

Now what about us? What might God want our church to do in response to this chapter? Our class? Ourselves?

 · · ● ● ·

Helps for leading your class or small group in learning from this chapter are located at the back of this book.

9 what next?

NINE WAYS TO IMPLEMENT THE IDEAS IN THIS BOOK

Mark and Carol considered themselves "freelance" Christians for much of their lives. Carol became a Christian in high school after she started attending a Christian athletic club, and Mark received Christ as a college freshman when a friend led him to the Lord. Throughout their college years, they attended church here and there, "wherever the best worship was." Their attendance was sporadic, but they made an effort to be in church whenever the service times didn't conflict with the soccer team's schedule or Mark's part-time job. The two were married in Carol's home church, which her parents still attend now and then.

When they took their first jobs and settled down in Omaha, Mark and Carol made an intentional decision to attend church occasionally but not frequently. It was then that they coined the term *freelance* to describe their spiritual lives. But over their first year of marriage, they both sensed something was missing. They had friends at work, but they yearned for something else—although they weren't sure what that might be.

Sometime later Angela invited Carol to visit her church. When Mark and Carol both found a free Sunday, they went. They enjoyed the experience and agreed to keep "dropping in" from time to time. Eventually, Mark and Carol joined one of the small groups, the same one attended by Angela. There they found a group of loving people, sharing one another's lives, "Just like our college buddies," as Mark put it. Group members often used the phrase "doing life together."

Over the following year, Mark and Carol became close friends with the other ten people in the group. They went skiing, did work projects, went out to eat after every Sunday service, and began to plan a mission trip that they could do as a group. Last night after Mark and Carol took their evening run together, Carol said, "It seems like we've found the real church hasn't it?"

"Yeah," Mark replied, trying to catch his breath. "Maybe this is what we were missing."

∘ ∘ ● ∘ ∘

So, What Next?

Each chapter in this book ends with practical tips and questions intended to steer a group toward applying the content of this book to itself and its church. So it makes sense that the book itself should end the same way. So, what next? If you agree with some (or much) of this book's content, what should your class or group do next?

This book runs against the grain of both our culture's values and the church's usual practice. In our individualistic culture, we tend to see everything as "all about me." This book calls for us to think about *we*. It calls us to see how the church *as a group* can grow spiritually. Having read or studied this book, you will most likely return to our culture's habitual individualism unless you do something intentional to resist it. This chapter suggests some actions—shifts in thinking, really—that will help us all remember the corporate means of grace that aid the spiritual formation of Christ in his body, the church.

1. Begin to Ask, "How Holy Are We?"

Begin to spend more of the energy that you now expend on examining yourself and your own spiritual life on examining the church and its corporate spiritual health. It isn't all about you; it's about us. So turn your introspective inclinations toward your church. How holy is your church? Does it look like the body of Christ? Does it show as a group the characteristics of Jesus? If Jesus is concerned about the whole bride, not just the individual "body part" that you represent personally, what does that bride look like? How can she be better prepared for the wedding? How can the church as a group become more like Christ? What needs to change? Ask the corporate holiness question.

That is not to say that you should abandon concern for individual holiness. Just be more evenhanded in thinking about holiness, considering the church's spiritual state along with your own. At the end of every Bible study, begin asking a new question that goes beyond personal application. Ask, "How should our church, as a group, apply this Scripture?" That will help guide you to a more balanced approach to holiness, one that includes both personal and corporate spirituality.

2. Quit Feeling Guilty about Christian Fellowship

God has ordained *koinonia* as a means of grace to make the church holy. So quit apologizing for spending time with other Christians, and refuse to let others shame you for it. But remember that fellowship is more than just hanging out together; it has the goal of making the church holy. Be intentional about seeing fellowship in that way. Turn conversations toward spiritual things, and make an effort to build up others during your fellowship times. Pizza itself will not make a church holy. But pizza eaten together and accompanied by conversation that is aimed at building, supporting, encouraging, and developing others will do that. Make your fellowship times with other Christians sanctified, set apart for making each other better Christians.

3. Treat Corporate Prayer as Seriously as Private Prayer

Who among us treats prayer at church as seriously as we do personal prayer? Very few of us do, probably. But why not? Shouldn't the prayers of the saints offered collectively matter more than our solo prayers at home? Of course they should. Start acting as if the prayers offered at church are really important. Instead of complaining about them, or snoozing through them, let God use those prayers as a means of grace to change and sanctify us. Even if some of the prayers are childish and sound more like announcements than prayers, begin opening your heart to them and expecting them to change you. Then, after you've allowed corporate prayer to change your group, you might suggest ways your church can make corporate prayer better and more effective as a sanctifying agent.

4. Consider Public Scripture Reading as a Means of Grace, Just like Personal Devotions

As you do with corporate prayer, treat Scripture reading at church as a corporate means of grace. Remind yourself every week that hearing the Scripture is one of God's means for making the church a holy church—by washing with the Word. Intentionally shift your mind-set so that you expect to receive life-changing power from the simple act of hearing Scripture. Abandon the thought that the only way to benefit from Scripture is to study it intensively. We can be changed by the Word of God by just hearing those words; we do not always have to study them. (Consider how preposterous it would be to take an hour to study the nuances of your lover saying, "I really do love you." Just hearing those words should be enough!) When the Scripture is read during a service, open your ears as a direct channel to your heart, not just your mind, and expect God to use his Word to change you. By treating Scripture as a channel for God's power, you will receive it in the same expectant manner that you receive the Lord's Supper. It will change you.

5. Expect a Movement of God

Expectancy among church members sometimes begins with one person or with a small group. Start expecting God to move in your church. Seek his moving, and wait on him. Share with others your hope, which will become infectious. You may have to wait only a few weeks, or you could wind up waiting for years, but don't give up! God always shows up. When he does, receive his changing grace, celebrate, and then spread the word. Expecting God to show up will not make him appear, but not expecting him can create an atmosphere of unbelief that will hamper his miraculous work among us. Become an expectant Christian.

6. Share Your Personal Testimony

Vow to seek opportunities to share with others what God has done in your life. Start with your small group meeting by adding your praise to the prayer requests. Share your stories with people you meet individually. When the whole church is ready to hear such reports, offer to glorify God with your story of his provision or care, remembering that such a testimony should be about God and not yourself. As a class or small group, do your part to make your church a place where God is expected to work because there are constant sightings of his work.

7. Receive the Lord's Supper as a Means of Grace for the Church

Quit approaching the Lord's Supper as if it were a funeral, and begin seeing this rite established by Christ as a mystical, life-changing means of grace. Train yourself so that every time you see the elements before the church, you expect to be changed in some way through eating and drinking them. Approach the meal with the specific characteristics of Christ that your church needs to develop firmly in mind. Then expect God to change his people through this sacrament. Testify to the change you personally experience through the Lord's Supper, and ask others about it. Little by little, you will see the church miraculously transformed as it receives this meal, believing that it really is what Christ intended it to be—a chief means of grace for sanctifying his church.

8. Find Ways to Witness Conversion and Baptism

Look for opportunities to see conversion happen. Even if your church doesn't make much of conversion, you can still do this in your class or group. When you hear of someone who has been converted, ask the person to come visit your group and tell about it, or at least be interviewed by you. Offer to hold a baptism party for new converts. Help them send invitations to their friends. Find ways to help your whole church witness the miracle work of God in forgiving and changing sinners, making them new creations. A church that has not witnessed a new birth for years may have forgotten how exciting this is. Reintroduce your church to this excitement whenever you have the opportunity. If nobody is converted through the ministries at your church . . . well, you may have to do the evangelism yourself!

9. Invest in Your Local Church

If there is one overriding theme in this book, it is the importance of the church—the local church where you attend—in God's plan to sanctify his people and accomplish his work in the world. This book is about the sanctification of God's people. I suspect someone from the younger generation will come along and write about the other half of the proposition: how the church does God's work in the world. That seems to be the emerging generation's special burden. But for now we should recognize that the church is founded by Christ himself and is God's chief means of making people holy. There are many good parachurch and non-church organizations that do wonderful things. But none of them were established by Christ for sanctifying his people and doing his work in the world. Our consumerist culture has misled us so that we treat even the church as a business and see ourselves as customers in search of a product or service. That way of thinking could not be further from the truth. If this book causes you to increase your commitment to the church, it will have accomplished its mission. There are dozens of ways you can invest in your local church, but three of them are essential: attend, give, and volunteer.

Attend Church More Often

As a sign of your commitment to the body of Christ, begin attending church more regularly than you have been, and perhaps begin attending one of the services that you usually skip. If being with the body helps us all become more like Christ, why not gather with the body more often? The early church met daily; we should be able to meet at least once a week, shouldn't we? Twice? Three times? More?

Give Money to Your Church

Habitually tithe (that is, donate 10 percent of) your income to your local church. It is true that giving to a local church seems rather boring. Many wonderful parachurch organizations spend millions of dollars to produce slick magazines and marketing videos touting their daring and idealistic missions. Meanwhile, your local church seems to take your giving for granted. Nevertheless, resist sending your core giving someplace other than Christ's church. Go ahead and send offerings to these other fine organizations, if you have an overabundance to give. But focus your core giving on the local church that preaches the Word, administers the sacraments, and is rightly organized according to the Scriptures.

Volunteer to Serve at Your Church

One of the reasons churches have to hire so many professional ministers today is that busy laypeople often can't afford to volunteer their time. Things that we once did as a service to Christ we now pay staff ministers to do as part of their jobs. This is not wrong, but it robs people of the joy of serving. Few of us get the same satisfaction from giving extra money to the church as we would from giving extra service. Every Christian ought to have at least two roles of service in the church, one major and one minor—say, teaching a class and serving as an usher. What are these for you? If you have more than two roles, then perhaps the time has come to recruit others and quit hogging the joy of service. But if you can't name two capacities in which you serve your church, it is probably time to start looking for your place to joyfully serve the body of Christ. If the church were just an organization needing volunteers, this wouldn't matter so much. But the church is the God-created body of Christ on earth, and participation by a real Christian is not optional.

Now what about us? What might God want our church to do in response to this chapter? Our class? Ourselves?

● ● ● ● ●

Helps for leading your class or small group in learning from this chapter are located at the back of this book.

study guide

How to Lead a Small Group in Learning from This Book

This book is about corporate spiritual disciplines, the means of grace God uses to sanctify his church. It makes sense, then, that it is best studied in community—in a small group or Sunday school class. The basic outline for leading a group in learning from this book includes these elements:

- Opening Caring and Sharing Time: Spend a few minutes catching up on one another's lives and praying together.
- Accountability: Ask everyone to report on what they did to begin applying last week's chapter. (This is a great time

to solicit personal testimonies.) Then ask how we see our church changing in the future.

- Teacher Introduction: Give a brief summary of important points from the current week's chapter.
- Bible Study: Read at least one of the Scriptures mentioned in this study guide, and deal with the questions that relate to it.
- Discussion: Select (or have group members suggest) questions from this section and discuss them with the group.
- Application and Reflection: Allow silence while each person writes a response to the final questions: "Now what about us? What might God want our church to do in response to this chapter? Our class? Ourselves?" Don't skip this part, ever. Invite members to announce their hopes or attempt to form "hope goals" as a group.
- Prayer: Pray together, asking God to direct your church's journey in becoming holy and to reveal himself during the next week.

It is important that you focus this book on practicing these disciplines and not merely studying them. Make the group about life change, not merely about gaining knowledge. Learning more about corporate prayer is nice, but it will be of little use unless you actually pray together more. Knowing about the value of Communion is not enough; Christians need to receive the Lord's Supper together expectantly. Be at peace with the idea that changes may come slower in some areas. This study introduces us to a variety of means of grace, and we can't focus on all of them all the time.

During your group's last session together, consider including a time where you consider your commitment to helping your entire church experience some of what you have learned. Until then, let each week be a wonderful exploratory time as you experiment with new ways of getting closer to God as a group. Let God transform your group first, then the entire church.

Chapter 1. The Bride

1. The opening story about Craig reminds us that there is a growing number of "churchless Christians" these days. Is Craig a real Christian? Can a person be a Christian but never gather with other Christians? How long can a person remain a Christian without connecting with other Christians? What is the church?

2. Read Ephesians 5:25–27. Without discussing marriage, make a list of everything this passage says explicitly about the church's relationship to Christ and about what has happened, is happening, and will happen between Christ and the church.

3. Read Revelation 21:2. To learn more about the church as a community, list the things we can learn from the analogy of a city that becomes a bride. In what ways should the church be like a city?

4. Read Ephesians 5:32–33 and Revelation 21:9. Paul ended the Ephesians 5 passage with the shocking statement that he wasn't really talking about husbands and wives after all, but about Christ and the church. This passage about submission, love, and care is often used primarily as an instruction for married couples and not as the basis for our theology of the church. Reread the entire passage, this time refusing to make it a recipe for healthy marriage but seeing it purely as a set of instructions on the sort of "wife" the church should be. Make a list of lessons you discover.

5. Read 1 John 4:12; Matthew 25:40; and Acts 9:4–5. These three passages were the key texts used by Augustine to refute the Donatists, a group who refused to be a part of the church and set out to found smaller, purer, gatherings of Christians. Discuss these questions after reading each Scripture:

- 1 John 4:12. What are the spiritual disciplines that help us love God better? Which ones help us to love others better? Which are we better at?
- Matthew 25:40. How could Christ claim that the way we treat our brothers and sisters is the way we treated him? Is it possible to treat Christ sweetly in our devotions yet spurn people at church? Why or why not?
- Acts 9:4–5. In what way did Paul persecute Jesus? When? How is that possible, since Paul had never met Jesus prior to his Damascus Road appearance?
- Taken together, what do these Scriptures indicate about where we would find Christ on earth today? What sobering thoughts does that raise for us?

6. This chapter strongly warns against the danger of privatized religion, attempting to correct today's imbalance in that direction. But just to be fair, list some of the dangers of communal religion, covenant theology, or placing too much emphasis on the church. Don't get too excited in making this list so that you don't reduce the impact of the book, but make it as a mental footnote to ponder again after reading this book. Any corrective can go too far, but that doesn't mean we should apply no corrective at all. After all, the reason we need the corrective is that the last corrective went too far!

7. If you've heard about personal and individual sanctification, tell what you know about it. What are the limitations and dangers of excessive emphasis on individual sanctification? Now switch sides. What could be the dangers of overemphasizing corporate sanctification? Which kind of sanctification does your church emphasize more? In which direction does the imbalance need to be corrected?

8. This chapter relies heavily on the wedding metaphor in order to minimize our individuality and elevate our corporate union as a church. The chapter lightly mentions the metaphors that picture the church as a city (above) and as a family. What other metaphors does the Bible use that emphasize the corporate nature of God's people? Are there metaphors for the church or for God's relationship to people that seem to emphasize individuality? Which metaphors are most popular in your church? Which metaphor, if any, is overused and needs to be balanced?

Chapter 2: Koinonia

1. Amy and Jason's trip to Haiti gave them a benchmark experience of Christian koinonia, or community. Amy wondered why the church couldn't be like that all the time. Make a list of the elements their mission trip included that most churches lack. This will be a recipe, of sorts, for helping the church find greater koinonia in its ongoing life.

2. Read Acts 1:14; 2:42–47; and 4:32. Without getting into a discussion of how appropriate it might be to practice communal life today, make a list of the things that characterized the common life of the early church in Acts. Focus on the internal "body life," not on the external effects. What was their life together

like? Once you've made the list, create a report card for your own church, assigning a grade for each item on the list. In which subjects did your church get an A? How many Cs did you get? How many Fs? Or perhaps they are all incompletes. Pick a single characteristic of common life that your church should improve, then decide how your group or class can help with that. Don't assign your ideas to other people, such as the pastor. Determine what your group can do to start becoming more like the early church.

3. Read Matthew 18:20. This chapter claims that whenever Christians gather in Christ's name, he is present automatically. We do not have to ask him to come; he is there. If this is so, what should we do differently when we are gathered "in his name"? What things do we usually do that seem contrary to this idea? Read the wider context of this passage: Matthew 18:12–20. What is the primary function of Christ's presence among his people according to this passage? Is it appropriate to apply his promise of presence for purposes other than correction? Can a church expect Christ's presence in worship or fellowship if it fails to discipline itself?

4. Read Colossians 3:12–14. Once we understand that we as a church have been given the ministry of Christ on earth, much of the Scripture comes alive in a fresh way. No longer are passages like this one seen as a set of rules for individuals, but they are seen as what they were intended to be: a description of group life. Based on this passage alone, make a series of statements describing a church that practices this Jesus-style ministry with one another. Which of the statements best characterizes your church right now? Which one does your church need more help with?

5. Read 1 Corinthians 5:9–11 and 2 Corinthians 2:5–8. Discuss the idea of "dis-fellowshipping" a Christian who refuses to submit to church discipline and insists on open and flagrant sinning. Why would the church do such a thing? What would be the goal? What effect do you think it might have had on the church in Corinth to tolerate the situation in which a man was sleeping with his father's wife? Why was withholding fellowship such a drastic action in those days? Would that be an effective means of discipline for churches in the present day? If not, what would be?

6. Do a major study. Divide the Gospels among those in your group who are willing to take on a large assignment, and ask each one to study Christ's earthly ministry and make a list of the things he did. Use one whole meeting to collate and merge the lists into a descriptive master list titled "Jesus' Ministry Then; Our Ministry Now."

Consult your pastor before taking the next steps. He or she may want to lead the process.

- Refine the list even further, then convert it to a survey by which church attendees can rate each item in answer to the question: "How well is our church doing at taking up the ministry of Jesus?" Attendees can be asked to rate the items on a scale from one to five.
- Administer the questionnaire.
- Compile the results as a class or small group, finding the average score for each item.
- Prepare a report that lists the items from highest ranking to lowest.
- Ask your pastor to consider preaching a sermon on the notion of taking up Jesus' ministry as a church.

- After your pastor's sermon, distribute the report of your findings to every attendee.
- Announce a strategy meeting to discuss future direction of the church's ministries.
- Lead an open discussion concerning which of Christ's ministries your church does best, asking people to give examples and testimonies.
- Lead a discussion on your next steps at taking up more of Christ's ministry. Let people speak aloud about which aspects of Christ's ministry they think the church should develop next. (Those may not be the items having the lowest scores. Sometimes the Spirit will lead a church to upgrade items that the church is already doing a mediocre job with.)
- Distribute the same survey again, but this time ask attendees to respond to this statement: "Rank the top five areas our church should develop as our next step in taking up the ministry of Christ."
- Compile the results and announce them to the church.
- Appoint a group to work with the pastor in brainstorming ideas for changing the values, allocating the budget, and designing the programming that will be needed in order to implement this plan.
- Create accountability for the church so that it will be sure to act on these resolutions.
- Allow at least one year for these changes to be implemented. Churches occasionally change in less than a year, but don't count on it.
- Revisit the list again after a year or so, and continue the process of becoming more and more like Christ!

Chapter 3: Corporate Prayer

1. The story of Travis and Kara illustrates two kinds of churches. While we might assume that they moved to a more conservative Protestant church, the story would be similar if they had attended an Eastern Orthodox church, where prayer is dominant in worship. Travis and Kara's former church, which downplayed prayer, typifies many evangelical churches. Why is this? Why would evangelical churches reduce the number of prayers and their significance in corporate worship? In all probability, Travis and Kara's first church was once very much like their second. What makes a church come to diminish prayer in worship? What replaces it?

2. Read Acts 4:23–31. This is the first extensive corporate prayer recorded for the New Testament church. List the differences you see between this prayer and most of our corporate prayers today. Do the same for the Lord's Prayer. Finally, make a list of the things you think we ought to change in our corporate praying, based on the insights gained from the Spirit as you made this study.

3. Read Ephesians 6:18. What is the difference between praying in the Spirit and praying some other way? What would you list as candidates for "all kinds of prayers and requests"? How can a church practically "keep on praying for all the saints"?

4. Read James 5:15–16. Tell about a healing service you attended, and its results. Why do you think confessing sins to one another is a part of this "order of worship" for a healing service? What connection does righteousness have with effective prayer? Aren't all Christians "righteous" in position, that is, by virtue of their right relationship with God? Or is James talking about

actual godliness, that is, being a truly holy person? Is the prayer of a godly Christian more effective than that of a carnal Christian?

5. Read Revelation 5:8 and 8:3–4. What does this portrayal of prayer in heaven tell us about prayer? Once the world ends, will there be no more prayer in heaven? Will we have nothing more to pray about? If you think there will be prayer in heaven, how will it be similar to or different from prayer today?

6. What is the connection between faith in God and prayer to God in your life? Was there a time in your life when your faith was weak or absent and your prayers were too? Now connect the two—faith and prayer—in the church. Is prayerlessness an indicator of our faithlessness?

7. If we made a list of the values illustrated by our practice of corporate prayer, what would that list include? How would that list compare with God's values? If Christ were to pray at our church, do you think he would pray in the same way we pray or differently?

8. List some of the different ways in which people pray. Without rejecting their approach or making fun of them, list the varied approaches to prayer you've observed. What is the strength of each?

9. How might we better respond to univocal prayers, such as the pastoral prayer?

10. Of all the ways of praying together, which appeals to you most? Least? Why? Which kinds of corporate prayer is your church already doing? Which ones could be improved? How?

Chapter 4: Scripture

1. Richard Smith, the visiting preacher mentioned at the start of this chapter, was correct; the first Christians heard the Word in worship. They did not read along in their own Bibles. Brooke was used to using her eyes as the port of entry for Scripture, rather than her ears. What would change for today's Christians if they only heard Scripture rather than reading it? How would the use of Scripture among us change? What things would we do less? What would we do more? Do you think that we ought to try things just because the early church did them? To what extent are we free to move beyond the practices of the early church? How far is too far?

2. Read 1 Timothy 4:13. Paul's instruction to Timothy lists three primary duties for this young pastor. List the occasions when your church does each of the three. Rate each of them. Which of the three does your church do best? Worst? Name several ideas for improving the area where you're weakest. As always, be careful not to berate the worship leaders in your church. Remember that these exercises are group assessments, not opportunities to accuse others of falling short. If you are tempted to blame, then switch to assessing whatever you are responsible for. If you have no responsibilities in the church, then ponder that fact to prepare yourself for evaluating others.

3. Read John 17:17. In his High Priestly Prayer, Jesus prayed for the church—both the apostles who were present and the church to come, including us. What did Jesus mean by asking the Father to sanctify the church? How do we know whether or not this prayer has been answered? What was the agent of sanctification here, the "soap" that God would use to cleanse his

bride? In what ways can God's Word sanctify the church, making it holy, Christlike? Can you give an example of a church that was changed—as a church—through God's Word? In what invisible ways is the church purified and sanctified by the Word?

4. Read Revelation 1:3. Who is "the one" in this verse, and who are "those who"? What do you think could be the blessing that this Scripture promises? Does this promise extend to all Scripture, or just the book of Revelation? Besides reading and hearing, what additional step is outlined in this passage that is important for the church?

5. Read Ephesians 5:25–27. Paul claimed that Christ died to make the church holy. We understand the idea that Christ died to save us personally from our sins, but what does it mean that Christ died for the church, not just for us personally? Christ is cleansing the church, purifying her as he makes her holy and spotless. Paul said Christ is doing this "by the washing with water through the word." As a group, look to the Holy Spirit to guide you in figuring out what this means and how it happens. What do the words *washing*, *water*, and *word* mean here? Don't just offer your personal opinions but seriously test the Holy Spirit's promise to lead your group into truth. See if the Holy Spirit—and not your own cleverness—can guide your group to discover what Jesus meant. Reflect on the process you just experienced. How is a Holy-Spirit-based, group process different from other approaches, such as hearing from a teacher who knows all, or thinkers who pool ignorance? How did your group find help from outside sources? Did some group members have more authority than others? Why?

6. Think back to a time when your church had a "gestalt Bible experience" that changed the entire church. Think of a

group study experience in which the whole was greater than the sum of the parts; that is, when because of a guest speaker's message, pastor's sermon, or series of teachings, the entire church—not just a majority of its members—was changed as a church. Try to recall sermons that seemed to change not just you personally but the entire church. Tell about it and about what changed in the church. In your discussion, try to identify what typifies the kind of preaching that changes a whole church.

7. Why is it that evangelical churches, which loudly claim to believe in the authority of the Bible, have so little Bible reading in their worship? What factors may have led us to develop this odd situation?

8. Make a list of "rules" for reading Scripture publicly, as if you were making a set of instructions for training a reader to serve in your church.

Chapter 5: Movement of God

1. The experience of Ian and Kelli is repeated a thousand times every week in evangelical churches. While many folk want to avoid the excesses of the charismatic movement, they hunger for God to move among his people from time to time. Beyond simply plotting the present position of your church on the expectation continuum, ask in which direction your church is moving. Is your church increasingly expectant about God's moving, or less so? What makes a church that once consistently experienced God's moving in dramatic ways gravitate away from this expectation? How can a church reverse the course of such a shift?

2. Read James 5:14–16. What are the elements of the order of service for this healing service outlined by James? Who is

supposed to be doing this praying? What do you think is the connection between confession of sin and healing? List some reasons why today's church is reluctant to deal with healing. List some reasons why we might give healing a greater place in our midst.

3. Read Acts 2:1–14 and 4:31. If you had been a witness to these two events, how would you describe each to your spouse when you got home? What observable, miracle-like things happened in connection with these events? Is the filling of the Spirit a repeatable event, or was it a one-time occurrence intended only to jumpstart the early church? What other Scripture passages speak of esoteric or ecstatic experiences in connection with God's work? What is the difference between a person being filled by the Spirit and a church being filled with the Spirit? Do you think there are differences in the ways a person might seek the filling of the Spirit and the ways a church might seek to be Spirit filled? Would you say that your church is a Spirit-filled church? Would you say that you are a Spirit-filled believer?

4. Read Acts 15:1–2. Use Acts 15 to answer the following questions: What incident triggered the need for a decision by the church leaders? What was the original two-part "motion" before the body? Who sponsored it? Outline possible arguments for both positions on this issue. What might have been the effect if this "motion" had passed? List the speakers against the motion and the essence of what they said. Describe how James suggested amending the "motion." How did the church leaders propagate their decision to the churches? If you had been on the "losing" side of this debate, what would you have done?

5. Some argue that God no longer shows up to perform miracles but did so only in earlier dispensations of history. What do you think of this notion and why?

6. It was stated that Christians nowadays simply have too much unbelief to receive many miracles from God. To find out whether you agree or disagree, draw a continuum on a sheet of paper with one end representing zero (no expectation of miracles) and the other representing one hundred (an atmosphere of total faith). Mark the place on that scale that represents your own faith. Where would you place the faith of your church? Your denomination? Your nation?

7. Were you ever healed, or have you witnessed an undeniably miraculous healing by God? Tell the story.

8. Have you ever attended a worship service during which God showed up so powerfully that you still remember it? Tell the story, and share how the event changed you.

9. Have you ever witnessed God showing up at a business meeting where an important decision was to be made, so that even after sharp disagreement between members, the decision was made in unity? Tell about it.

10. What are the dangers that could accompany applying the principles discussed in this chapter? What excesses could result from taking this chapter too seriously? What safety measures would guard against these dangers?

Chapter 6: Testimony

1. The story of Burt illustrates how a person from a different background could be simultaneously put off and fascinated by personal testimony. How might a church keep from alienating people when using personal testimony? What about the other type of people—the ones who have seen an overemphasis on personal testimony and now reject it as part of their "fundamentalist

upbringing"? How might a church help people who have been burned by personal testimony rediscover its usefulness?

2. Read Acts 7:1–2. Study all of Acts 7 in order to outline Stephen's mighty-acts story. What did he leave out that you would add as a critical element of God's redemption story? What events from the New Testament or from church history would you add to Stephen's story, extending it to show God's mighty acts up to the present day?

3. On what basis do we believe in the resurrection of Jesus, other than personal testimony? Which of the two God concepts— God-as-distant or God-as-nearby—do you lean toward personally? Admit it to the group. Tell some stories of excesses or errors you've seen in testimonies in the past. How might these errors be avoided in future use of the testimony? Are there any abuses of the testimony that professional ministers or musicians are prone to in their preaching or worship leading? How might these be avoided? On a scale from zero to one hundred, how would you rate your church's expectancy quotient? That is, how much does your church expect God to work in the daily lives of its people? How would you rate churches that you have previously attended? Is there a right number, in your opinion? Would you like to hear more testimonies in your church? If so, when?

4. Test your knowledge of communal stories. How many of the conversion stories of people in the room can you retell? Count them. Of whom in your church can you recount a story of healing? If you were to retell a story of someone receiving power from God to overcome a sin or addiction, whose story would you tell? Can you name a story about a marriage being saved involving anyone from your church? Whose story of being filled with the Spirit do you know? What stories can you

name involving God's miraculous provision for people in need among your church members? From the story of your church's history, can you recount an instance in which a revival movement altered the course of your church? Can you tell the story of a time when God provided for your church when church members could not provide for themselves?

5. Share your testimony with your class or small group. Tell the story of how you became a Christian. Tell of a time when you saw an undeniably miraculous healing by God. Tell about how God delivered you from a particular sinful practice. Tell of how your marriage was healed by God. Tell the story of how God provided for or protected you miraculously. Tell about when you saw a God-sent revival take place. Tell the story of a great ingathering, a time when many folk found Christ over a brief period of time. Tell the story of the Holy Spirit's filling you and transforming your life as a Christian. What other stories should you tell as part of your own testimony?

Chapter 7: The Lord's Supper

1. What do you think of Faith's story? Can taking Communion really change us—sanctify us of wrong thoughts, attitudes, or actions? How is going to the altar to seek God's help through prayer different from going forward to receive the Lord's Supper? Is Communion a means of grace only to those who receive it believing that it is? What role did belief play in Faith's seeing changes in her life?

2. Read 1 Corinthians 11:20–22. How is it possible that the Lord's Supper deteriorated to such a mess in this church? Imagine the stages of decline that may have led to this disastrous end. What would have been the first steps toward such a disaster? Do

you think the church today is taking dangerous baby steps regarding its practice of the Lord's Supper? Given their trajectory, what eventual results are possible?

3. Read 1 Corinthians 11:23–25. Most Bible scholars agree that Paul wrote these words before any of the Gospels were written, thus they are among the earliest recorded words of Christ. What do you think Paul meant when he claimed that he "received" something and delivered it to the Corinthian Christians? What did he receive? The first Christians took these words to mean they should practice Communion every time they gathered. Later on, especially during the Middle Ages, the Roman Catholic Church ceased offering Communion regularly. Since the Reformation, there has been a consistent ebb and flow in the frequency of Communion: Often it rises in times of renewal and becomes infrequent in times of secularization, when nominal Christianity prevails. In your opinion, what is the right frequency for offering Communion? List some ways that the church can provide Communion for those who want it more frequently, other than scheduling it as part of the primary weekly worship services.

4. Read 1 Corinthians 11:26–29. Find all three tenses of Communion—past, present, and future—in the first phrase of verse 26. Describe the difference between being unworthy and drinking in an unworthy manner. What were the Corinthians doing that caused their practice of Communion to be done unworthily? We are perhaps far from being in danger of practicing Communion as unworthily as the Corinthians did, but Paul here issued sharp instructions for his readers and teaches all of us something about the importance of Communion. Describe this.

5. Read John 6:53–56. This hard saying of Jesus has sometimes been interpreted to be about something other than the

Lord's Supper. Try to think of other possible interpretations for this saying and explain them. Now interpret the saying purely as a reference to the Lord's Supper. What does it mean if it applies to taking Communion? In your opinion, which interpretation seems most likely to be correct?

6. Most churches expect a minister to officiate at the Lord's Supper. This practice is rooted in the fear of seeing the abuses that occurred in the past when serving Communion was delegated to anyone who wanted to perform it. What is your church's view on this? Can family members serve Communion to themselves at a Thanksgiving or Christmas dinner, without a minister present? What would be the advantages and dangers of such a practice?

Chapter 8: Conversion and Baptism

1. Pastor Brent's approach to conversion is not unique in the evangelical church, which has increasingly rejected revivalistic approaches that call for instantaneous conversion and has adopted more gradual models of evangelism. It is easy to see pastors as responsible for this, but ask yourself how the laity might have contributed to the decline in expectation of instantaneous conversion. Has God shifted the way he works with people so that a gradual process is now his norm for conversion? If people are converted gradually, when are they ready for baptism? How does the role of baptism change when instantaneous conversion begins to wane?

2. The process of conversion was presented in this order in this chapter: conviction, conversion, baptism, study and training, and church membership. Do you know of other churches that consider conversion as happening in a different sequence? How

was the order of conversion different in the first-century church? In the church of A.D. 100?

3. Some say the church itself is an evangelist, meaning that the church's mere existence in a secular world is a witness to the gospel and that our presence draws people to Christ. If a person was to wake up one morning in your town and feel the need to find God, would he or she know where to go? Most of us assume that person would go to a church, and this notion frees some churches to be lighthouse churches, standing firm as a warm haven for those who want peace with God. Other churches consider themselves lifesaving stations whose members go out to rescue lost people and bring them back to shore. Which model do you lean toward personally? Which model is more like your church?

4. The three traditional meanings of baptism are: a confession of faith, washing from sin, and death to the old life. How do you see these three aspects of baptism played out in the conversion of a person? Can you recall Scripture that illustrates each one? Which of the three does your church emphasize more?

5. Search the following Scripture passages and discover everything you can about baptism. What new discoveries did you make alone or as a group?

- Matthew 3:13–16
- Matthew 28:19–20
- Mark 16:15–16
- John 3:1–5
- Acts 2:38–41
- Acts 8:26–40
- Acts 22:16

- Romans 6:3–5
- Galatians 3:26–27
- Ephesians 4:4–5
- Colossians 2:12
- Titus 3:5
- 1 Peter 3:21

Chapter 9: What Next?

1. Why do you think Mark and Carol didn't feel the need to be connected to a church while they were in college?

2. What makes it so hard for people to break into the sort of fellowship that Mark and Carol found in their small group? What do groups do that makes it hard for newcomers to join? How do people like Mark and Carol make it difficult for themselves to break in?

3. This book sets out the ideal: what a church would be if it were operating as God intended. Yet we all know many churches—probably most churches—fall far short of this ideal. The danger in describing the ideal church is the same as the danger in describing an ideal Christian. It sets a standard so high that no one can meet it and discourages people from even trying. What steps can your group take to ensure that this study does not cause you to give up on your church and seek another church that seems closer to the ideal? What steps or agreements can your group make to steer all of you toward constructive mending of the church?

4. Of all the ideas in this book, which ones are easiest for the pastor to implement and which are best started by a small group or by an individual?

5. Using this book's table of contents as a guide, make a self-assessment tool to grade the various corporate means of grace. For each, give three grades: one for your local church, one for your group or class, and one for yourself as an individual. What single action might be the first baby step toward improving the lowest grades? How might you leverage the higher grades to become even better at what you already do well?

6. This book selected only a few of the many corporate means of grace to examine. What are some of the other corporate means of grace that God uses to change us as a group? List them, and pretend you are outlining your own book or study for others—what would you say about them if your group were writing a book?

7. This book has delivered the clear message that the church should be the church. The church does not exist for itself alone, but also for the world. Just as an individual is a channel of God's grace to others, so the church is a channel of God's grace to the world. Others, probably writers from the emerging generation, may come along to write a similar book on how the church is an agent of grace in the world. If your group were to make the chapter titles for such a "missional" book, what would they be?

8. For you, what is the breakthrough truth from this book that will change the way you live?

9. As a group, name the ways that God has changed you—all together—through this study?

10. Now think of your local church. Has anything changed since you began this study? What? How? What do you expect to change next? Why? What step will you take to cooperate with the changes God wants to make in your church?

11. What are the primary Scriptures from this study that the Holy Spirit has brought alive for your group? In what ways have you come alive because of them?